Buyer Concentration, Market Structure, and Seller Profitability

A Reprint of a Dissertation Titled

THE RELATIONSHIP BETWEEN SELLER AVER-AGE PROFITABILITY AND MARKET STRUC-TURE, INCLUDING BUYER CONCENTRATION, IN UNITED STATES MANUFACTURING INDUSTRIES

Douglas Brooks

THE RELATIONSHIP BETWEEN SELLER AVERAGE PROFITABILITY

AND MARKET STRUCTURE, INCLUDING BUYER CONCENTRATION,

IN UNITED STATES MANUFACTURING INDUSTRIES

by

DOUGLAS GORDON BROOKS

A dissertation submitted in partial fulfillment

of the requirements for the degree of

DOCTOR OF BUSINESS ADMINISTRATION

UNIVERSITY OF WASHINGTON

1971

Approved by _____
            (Chairman of Supervisory Committee)

Department ___Marketing, Transportation, and International Business___
            (Departmental Faculty sponsoring candidate)

Date _____August 18, 1971_____

University of Washington

Abstract

THE RELATIONSHIP BETWEEN SELLER AVERAGE PROFITABILITY

AND MARKET STRUCTURE, INCLUDING BUYER CONCENTRATION,

IN UNITED STATES MANUFACTURING INDUSTRIES

by Douglas Gordon Brooks

Chairman of Supervisory Committee: Professor John C. Narver
Department of Marketing,
Transportation, and
International Business

There is an extensive body of theory in Economics and Industrial
Organization that relates market structure to the magnitude of seller
economic profits. High levels of market (seller) concentration and high
barriers to entry, combining in the extreme to yield a "perfect" monopoly,
are assumed to result in the long run in high profits, while low concentration and barriers, yielding at the other extreme perfect competition,
result in the long run in little or no economic profits. Although these
theoretical relationships are seldom challenged, particularly in their
extremes, empirical attempts at demonstrating them have resulted in disappointingly low levels of statistical significance and occasionally
contradictory results, and the strength of their conclusions have therefore suffered.

It is suggested in this dissertation that a problem with all previous studies relating market structure to seller profitability has been
the lack of control for variations in important market structure variables.
The most important exclusion has been the control for variations in the
buyer concentration facing the sellers in an industry. A measure for

buyer concentration is derived using the 1963 Input-Output tables, and this measure is shown to have a significant downward effect on seller profitability. In addition, its inclusion in a regression analysis is shown to have a substantial effect on the significance level of the variables controlling for variations in seller concentration, allowing the effects of seller concentration on seller profitability to be determined much more precisely than is possible in the absence of a measure for buyer concentration. Since buyer and seller concentration have effects on seller profitability that are opposite and roughly equal, the exclusion of one of these variables in a regression obscures the effects of the other.

In addition, the usual control variable for barriers to entry, the advertising to sales ratio, is shown to be an inappropriate surrogate for barriers to entry, and an adjustment to that measure, reflecting advertising intensity in consumers goods markets, is proposed. The regression results suggest that the adjusted advertising measure is a much more apporpriate surrogate for barriers to entry than is the usual measure.

The empirical analysis in this dissertation is carried out at the 2-digit SIC level of industrial aggregation, the level at which previous studies have generally been most successful. Some problems with empirically relating market structure to seller profitability at lower levels of aggregation are discussed, but no attempt is made to determine what the effects might be of introducing a control variable for variations in buyer concentration at these levels.

ii

TABLE OF CONTENTS

Chapter   Page

    I   INTRODUCTION AND SUMMARY   1

   II   THEORETICAL BACKGROUND AND RESULTS OF PREVIOUS STUDIES . . .   4

            Theoretical Relationships   5
              Effects of Seller Concentration   7
              Barriers to Entry and Seller Concentration   15
              Effects of Buyer Concentration   16
              Profits vs. Rate of Return   20

            Market Structure and Profitability   21
              Nature of Previous Findings   21
              Explanation of the Variation in Results   24

            Footnotes   35

  III   THEORETICAL MODEL AND MEASUREMENT OF DATA   40

            Buyer and Seller Concentration   41
            Barriers to Entry   52
            Growth of Market Demand   56
            Risk   57
            Industry Size   58
            Final Model   60

            Footnotes   62

   IV   EMPIRICAL RESULTS   65

            Footnotes   76

    V   CONCLUSIONS AND DISCUSSION   77

            Conclusions and Implications   78
            Review of Assumptions   79
            Areas for Future Research   85
            Footnotes   87

Bibliography   88

Appendices   94

    I   Distribution of Output for the Industries Used in the
           Analysis   95

   II   Two-Way Correlations Between the Variables Used in the
           Analysis   97

  III   Mathematical Note   98

   IV   Basic Data Used in the Analysis . . . . 103 iii

LIST OF FIGURES

Figure		Page
2-1	Industry Total Cost and Total Revenue Curves With Price Vectors OP_1 and OP_2	9
2-2	Demand Curves Facing Oligopolist X Depending on Whether Other Firms in the Industry Matxh X's Price Changes	13
3-1	Relationship Between the Partial Derivation of Seller Profitability With Respect to Seller Concentration For Constant Buyer Concentration	43
3-2	Relationship Between the Partial Derivation of Seller Profitability With Respect to Seller Concentration as a Function of Seller and Buyer Concentration	44
3-3	Relationship Between the Partial Derivative of Seller Profitability With Respect to Buyer Concentration as a Function of Seller and Buyer Concentration	44
3-4	The Partial Derivatives of Seller Profitability With Respect to Seller and Buyer Concentration For the Model $P=a+b(SC)+c(BC)+d(BC/SC)$	46
4-1	Partial Derivatives of Equation (9) With Respect to Seller and Buyer Concentration Over the Range of the Data For Seller Concentration	75

LIST OF TABLES

Table		Page
4-1	Regressions of Seller Rate of Return on Various Market Structure Variables (Equations (1) to (6))	69
4-2	Effects of Alternative Measures of Buyer Concentration . . .	70
4-3	Regressions of Seller Rate of Return on Alternative Formulations of the Model (Equations (6) to (12))	72

iv

ACKNOWLEDGMENT

The people who have befriended and helped me these last three years are far too numerous to list here, and a one-paragraph acknowledgment hardly gives justice to their contributions. Included in the list would be the faculty and staff of the School of Business Administration at the University of Washington, and especially Professors Alberts, Scott, and Tamura, who so willingly gave of their time and experience on my Supervisory Committee. A very special thanks goes to John C. Narver, Chairman of my Supervisory Committee, whose help and direction has been invaluable. A special thanks also goes to my wife, Alice, whose faith, thoughtfulness, and encouragement allowed me to continue in the program. Finally, James Makens, of the University of Dallas, unknowingly provided the catalyst that ultimately resulted in this dissertation late one evening in early 1968.

{This page intentionally blank)

CHAPTER I

INTRODUCTION AND SUMMARY

There is an extensive body of theory in Economics and Industrial Organization that relates market structure to the magnitude of seller economic profits. High levels of market (seller) concentration and high barriers to entry, combining in the extreme to yield a "perfect" monopoly, are assumed to result in the long run in high profits, while low concentration and barriers, yielding at the other extreme perfect competition, result in the long run in little or no economic profits. Although these theoretical relationships are seldom challenged, particularly in their extremes, empirical attempts at demonstrating them have resulted in disappointingly low levels of statistical significance and occasionally contradictory results, and the strength of their conclusions have therefore suffered.

This dissertation suggests that the relationship between variations in market structure, and in particular, seller concentration, and seller profitability is, in fact, quite strong, and would have been exposed more decisively by previous researchers if the correct control variables, and if an appropriate model, had been used. If we wish to detect the relationship between variations in seller concentration and seller profitability, variations in seller profitability caused by other factors <u>must</u> be controlled. But very few variables are controlled in most studies, and, in particular, no previous study has controlled for the effects of variations in the level of buyer concentration facing sellers in the industries used in the analyses. It is suggested herein that the effects of both seller and buyer concentration on seller profitability are substantial, but that they have nearly equal and opposite effects. Accordingly, the exclusion of buyer concentration has in large part led to the generally inferior results previously obtained.

Buyer concentration is shown to be a theoretically and empirically important element of market structure. The regression coefficient associated with buyer concentration, in the regression analysis used herein, is significant at the .005 level of significance, and the inclusion of buyer concentration in the model increases the t-value associated with the coefficient for seller concentration by almost 30% (from 5.0 to 6.5). Almost 90% of the variation in seller rate of return is explained by the market structure elements employed in the model.

In addition, the usual control variable for barriers to entry, the advertising to sales ratio, is shown to be an inappropriate surrogate for barriers to entry, and an adjustment to that measure, reflecting advertising intensity in consumers goods markets, is proposed. The regression results suggest that the adjusted advertising measure is a much more appropriate surrogate for barriers to entry than is the usual measure.

The dissertation proceeds as follows: in Chapter II, the theory relating market structure (and in particular buyer and seller concentration) to seller profitability is formulated. The results of previous studies are discussed, along with the suggested reasons for the non-uniformity of the conclusions drawn. In Chapter III, the model used for analysis is developed, as is the methodology for quantifying the variables employed in the analysis. Chapter IV provides the results of the empirical analysis, along with comparisons of the type of results that would have been obtained had more traditional models been employed. Finally, Chapter V discusses the significance of the results, suggests some areas for further study, and raises important issues that might reflect on the validity of the results obtained herein.

CHAPTER II

THEORETICAL BACKGROUND AND RESULTS OF PREVIOUS STUDIES

In this chapter we will formally develop the theory relating market structure to seller average profitability. We will then summarize the empirical attempts at demonstrating this relationship, paying special attention to the conflicting nature of the findings and of the conclusions drawn. Some explanations for the conflicting results will be offered.

Theoretical Relationships

Economic theory is quite precise about the relationship between price and profits (in the economic sense) in a purely competitive industry: price adjusts in the long run so that no economic profits are available, and the rate of return earned by all the firms equals the risk-adjusted cost of capital. The theory is equally precise about what would happen if one firm bought all the others, thus creating a monopoly: if he were able to foreclose all possible new entry, the monopolist would cut back output and raise prices, earning a "monopoly profit" in excess of the cost of capital. It would seem reasonable, therefore, that the total industry economic profit would be functionally related to the number of firms in the industry and would vary from the monopoly profit to zero as the structure of the industry varied from purely monopolistic to purely competitive. If otherwise, there must be some magic number of firms above which no economic profits are earned and below which monopoly profits are earned.

Industrial Organization suggests that the "degree of monopoly," as measured sometimes by the number of firms, but more appropriately by the concentration ratio -- i.e., the percentage of industrial output accounted for by, say, the four largest producers in the industry -- is but one of the important structural elements that affect market profitability. Market structure is defined, simply, as "those characteristics of the organization of a market which seem to influence strategically the nature of competition and pricing within the market."[1] Caves lists the elements of market structure, in his order of importance, as

1. (seller) concentration
2. product differentiation
3. barriers to the entry of new firms
4. growth rate of market demand
5. price elasticity of market demand
6. ratio of fixed to variable costs in the short run.[2]

Although the meaning of most of these elements should be clear to the reader, two of them deserve some elaboration. Product differentiation refers to the degree to which buyers perceive differences in the offerings of the producers in the same product market. Thus, perfect differentiation would be the polar opposite of perfect homogeneity.[3] Barriers to entry, however, as Bain views them, are

> The advantages of the established sellers in an industry over potential entrant sellers, these advantages being reflected in the extent to which established sellers can persistently raise their prices above a competitive level without attracting new firms to enter the industry.[4]

An important element of market structure not included in Caves' list is buyer concentration -- the percentage of total market output purchased by, say, the largest four buyers. The purpose of this dissertation is to show that buyer concentration is, indeed, an important element of market structure, and to show how buyer concentration interrelates with seller concentration to affect seller profitability.

Caves points out that the importance of market structure lies in the way that it influences the conduct of firms in the market.

> Market conduct consists of a firm's policies toward its product market and toward the moves made by its rivals in that market . . . To simplify . . . we shall divide market conduct into three major areas of business policy:
>   1. Policies toward setting prices
>   2. Policies toward setting the quality of the product
>   3. Policies aimed at coercing rivals.[5]

Thus, the structure of a market influences the conduct of firms within that market, and the structure and conduct together influence the performance of firms in the market.

Of particular importance here is how structure, and the conduct resulting from that structure, influences the profitability of firms in a market. In a purely competitive market structure, conduct and profit performance are determinant -- i.e., sellers have no discretion over price and in the long run there will be no economic profits. In a monopoly, given a firm goal of profit maximization (and blockaded entry), sellers have discretion over price, but there is a unique price at which profits are maximized -- it is the price which results in an output at which marginal cost equals marginal revenue.

Effects of Seller Concentration

But economic theory is quite imprecise about the nature of the relationship between structure and profitability if the structure is neither purely competitive nor monopolistic.[6] In Industrial Organization it is often hypothesized[7] that the average profit level, P, in an industry is a function of the "degree of monopoly" as measured by the concentration ratio (ceteris paribus). Since, in a purely competitive industry the concentration ratio would be zero, and in a monopoly the concentration ratio would be 1.0, the relationship between the rate of return, R, which reflects both profits and the cost of capital, and concentration might be described by the linear model

$$R = a + b(\text{Concentration})$$

where a is the purely competitive rate of return and b is the maximum level of economic profit available to a monopolist.

The theoretical justification for this type of model is as follows: consider the Total Cost (TC) and Total Revenue (TR) curves shown in Figure 2-1. (For simplicity it has been assumed that Marginal Cost, MC, equals zero. A relaxation of this assumption has little consequence for the following argument.) Marginal Cost and Marginal Revenue (MR) at any point, Q, are represented by the slopes of the TC and TR curves, respectively, at that point. If the industry is a monopoly, a profit maximizing monopolist will set price and output at the point where MC=MR, or the point at which the TR curve is horizontal (since MC has been assumed equal to zero). The vector OP_1 represents the profit maximizing monopoly price, and P_1A represents the maximum monopoly profits earned at that price.

Now suppose the industry is an oligopoly consisting of, say, three firms, each with identical cost functions and all producing a product which is perfectly homogeneous (i.e., consumers perceive that the products of all three offer the same utility and therefore there is no product differentiation).[8] Let each have, initially, an equal share of the

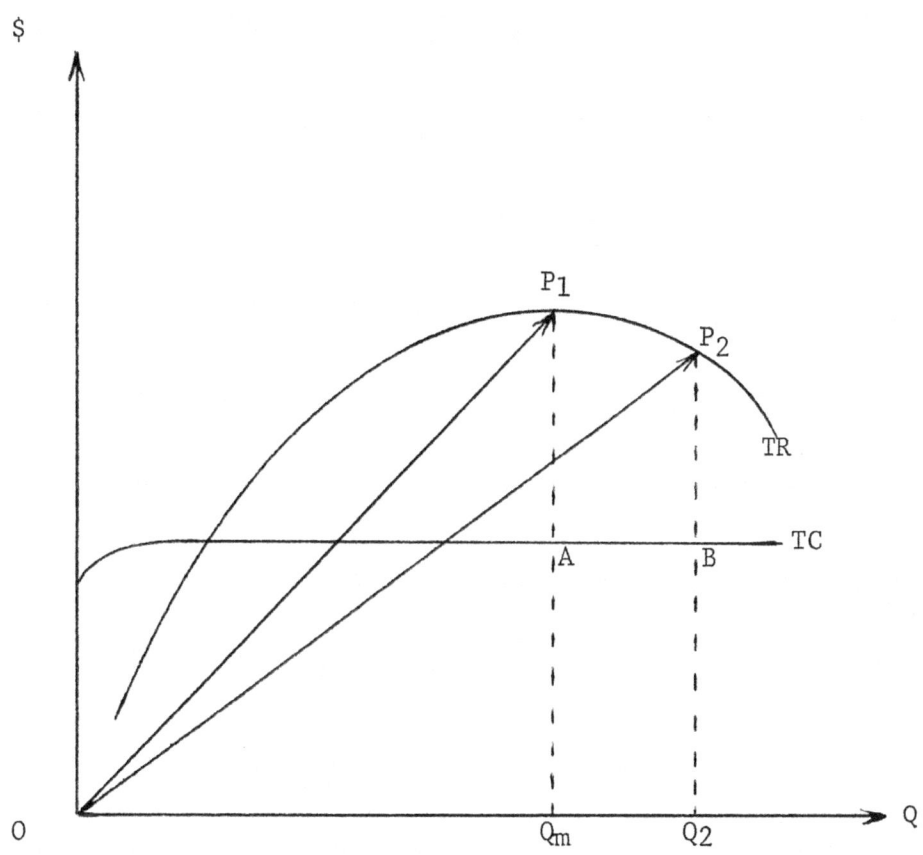

Figure 2-1

Industry Total Cost and Total Revenue
Curves With Price Vectors OP_1 and OP_2

market equal to $Q_m/3$. Let the industry profit maximizing price still be represented by OP_1. No goods can be sold at a price greater than OP_1, for if oligopolist X, for example, raises his price above OP_1, his customers will switch their patronage to either Y or Z. If X, however, lowers his price, say to OP_2, and if Y and Z do not follow, X can attract customers from Y and Z, expand his market share, and though total industry profits will decrease, his will increase at the expense of Y and Z, for X's demand curve is highly elastic if Y and Z maintain their prices at the level OP_1.

But if Y and Z lower their price in order to maintain their market shares and at least a portion of the profits that would otherwise be lost to X, the market shares will remain stable at the previous level, and the price for the product will be OP_2. Total output has increased to Q_2, but total industry profits have decreased from P_1A to P_2B. Furthermore, no one firm can now unilaterally increase price in order to regain the previous level of profit. The three firms can regain the point of maximum profit only if they coordinate their actions and all raise prices together, agreeing to maintain the previous price level.

The action undertaken by X in this model, that of lowering price to OP_2, was irrational, for Y and Z were compelled to follow. Thus, a profit maximizing oligopolist would have recognized that such an action would ultimately lead to lower overall profits. But it was an irrational move only as a result of several of the assumptions of the model: (1) profit maximizing motives, (2) homogeneous products, (3) perfect information, and (4) similar cost functions. If X, for example, had established a goal of sales maximization (subject perhaps to some satisfactory level of profit), rather than profit maximization, his move would have been a rational one to take. The only recourse open to the profit maximizers Y and Z in this case would be to try to "discipline" X by means of a price war in order to "persuade" him to cooperate and maintain the monopoly price, OP_1.

Even if all firms are profit maximizers, however, if we relax our assumptions of perfect information and product homogeneity in our example above, allowing for some degree of product differentiation, X may feel that by lowering his price from the industry optimum price OP_1 to OP_2 he would (1) gain enough in market share at the expense of each of the others that his overall profits would increase, but (2) the loss in profits to each of the others would not be sufficient to motivate them to retaliate with lower prices themselves. Y and Z could feel that the loss in profits was negligible and be willing to let X "get away" with his actions, or, since Y and Z face different demand curves than X (since we have allowed for some degree of product differentiation), a price cut sufficient to meet X's price may result in lower overall profits in spite of that portion of profits regained from X.

If X's assessment of Y's and Z's reactions is correct, then a unilateral price cut is a rational action, and could lead to higher profits for X. But if X were wrong in his assessment, his action would lead to lower prices everywhere, and lower economic profits for all firms. Thus, an intendedly rational, but fallible, profit maximizer could take actions that would ultimately lead to lower, not maximal, industry profits in an imperfect world.

The reader will recognize that the above discussion really relates to the idea of a "kinked demand curve."[9] In Figure 2-2, let D_1 be the demand curve facing X assuming that all the firms in the industry change their prices together. P_1 and Q_1 represent the profit maximizing point in this case. (It is the point of unit elasticity along D_1 since we have assumed that MC=0.) If firm X feels that it can increase profits by lowering its price to P_2, for the reasons described above, then the demand curve perceived by firm X is that labeled D_{x_1}. If the other firms in the industry do not follow, X can maximize profits at P_2 and Q_{2a}; but if the other firms do follow X's price cut, the new equilibrium point will be at P_2 and Q_{2b}, which is not, of course, optimal.

The optimum, profit maximizing point can now be regained if all firms raise their prices back to P_1. But if each firm, for example firm X, now perceives his demand curve as D_{x_2}, no firm will be willing to take the first step and initiate the increase, for in doing so he will feel that he will lose a disproportionate share of the market to his rivals. Thus, only through the coordinated efforts of all firms can the price be readjusted to the profit maximizing level.

It is important to note that requirement for coordinated activity does not just apply to the case in which the action of one rival has precipitated a general price decline. If virtually any disturbance occurs -- for example a shifting of the demand curve, a change in the cost functions, etc. -- which results in the current price being lower than the industry optimum one, the coordinated activity of all rivals is necessary in order for the industry to adjust to the new optimum point.

It is appropriate to ask what forms this coordination will take. Bain identifies several broad forms of coordination:

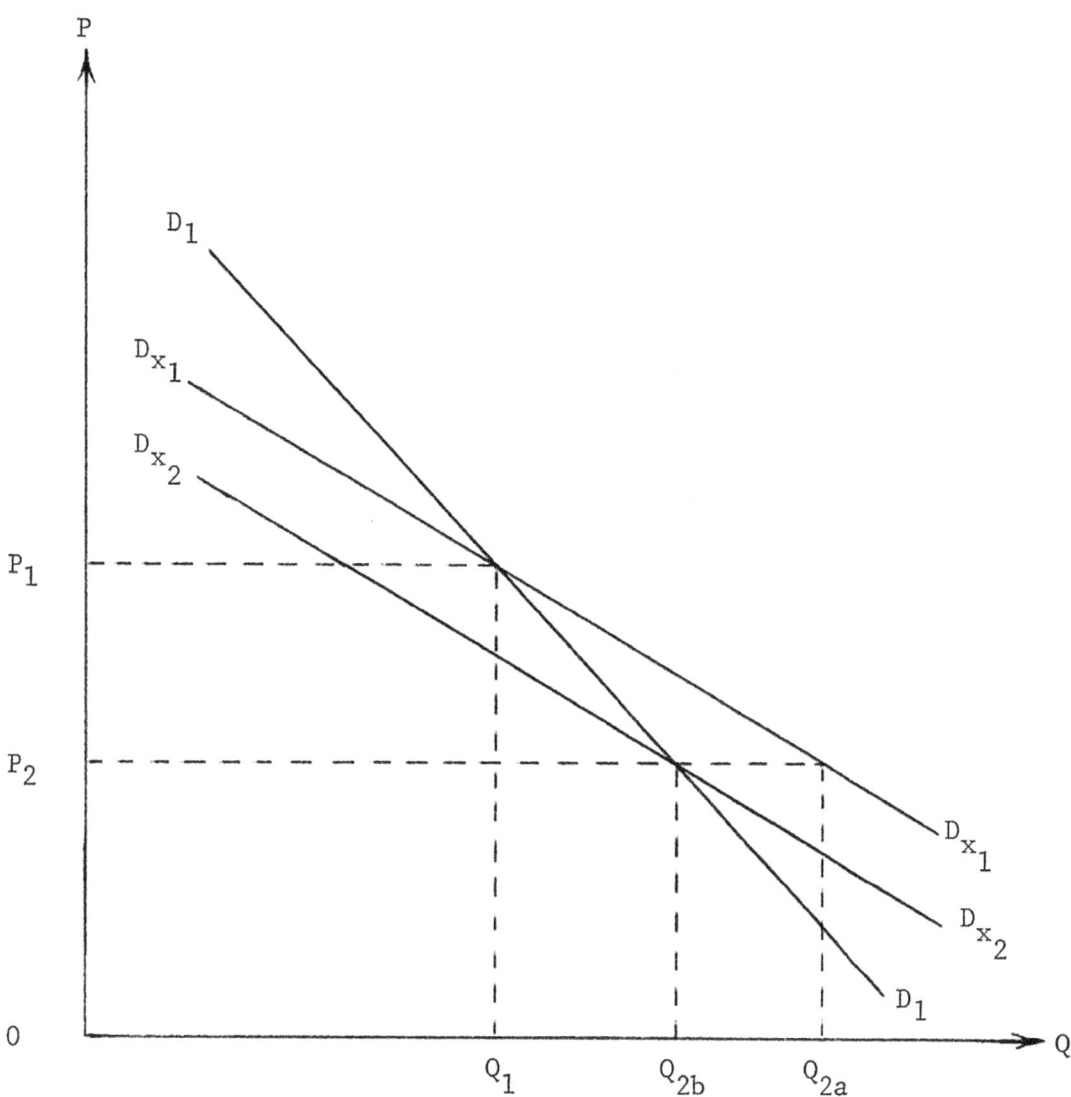

Figure 2-2

Demand Curves Facing Oligopolist X Depending
On Whether Other Firms in the Industry
Match X's Price Changes

1. direct agreement between sellers
2. price leadership
3. common "rules of behavior"
4. various forms of "implicit" agreement.[10]

Whatever form the coordination takes, it will be more or less perfect (in the sense of maximizing industry profits) depending on the structure of the industry. Bain suggests that

> There are some minimal structural conditions for the emergence and survival of complete collusion (perfect coordination) as a pattern of market conduct. The most important of these -- a necessary but not sufficient condition -- is that the number of sellers in the industry shall be sufficiently small, and the degree of seller concentration sufficiently high, that it is feasible for agreements including all sellers to be arrived at, and further that there is a reasonable probability that all of the sellers will abide rigorously by the agreement. Agreements are practically impossible to arrive at if the number of sellers is large and unwieldy. Further, for agreements (if arrived at) to be viable, in the sense that all participants observe their terms, the individual sellers must be few enough, and control large enough individual market shares, that the defection of any one of them from the terms of the agreement would perceptively affect the welfare of his rivals, and invite attention and retaliation. Lacking this prerequisite, collusion if attempted will generally be unstable or imperfect.[11]

As seller concentration increases, ceteris paribus, coordination between sellers becomes easier and more effective -- i.e., the price can be more easily adjusted to, or maintained at, the profit maximizing level. Thus, the greater the seller concentration the higher should be the industry average profitability.

On the other hand, as seller concentration decreases, the effect of one seller on any of his rivals will diminish.

> The effects on other sellers of a given adjustment
> by one seller is smaller, and the probability of re-
> actions to small adjustments correspondingly less.
> In other words, interdependence is less intense, and
> there is more room for and probability of independent
> adjustments which neglect rivals' reactions.[12]

Thus, as seller concentration decreases we would expect that there would

be less interdependence among firms, firms would be less concerned with

industry profit maximization, and coordination would give way to competi-

tion. Price would then approach that which would be expected under pure

competition, and average industry profitability would correspondingly de-

crease. We can therefore hypothesize that interfirm competition will be

negatively correlated with, and industry average profitability will be

positively correlated with, seller concentration.

Barriers to Entry and Seller Concentration

An important condition that is not mentioned in the above develop-

ment is the condition of entry. Is it likely that high seller concen-

tration and high profits can coexist without restricted entry, since

economic theory suggests that high profits will attract new entrants,

thus lowering profits? Thus isn't seller concentration correlated with,

and possibly even a surrogate for, barriers to entry? Bain says no:

> We conclude that the correlation between the condi-
> tion of entry and the degree of seller concentration
> is sufficiently imperfect that each dimension of
> structure should be awarded separate and independent
> importance in making a structural classification of
> industries.[13]

Later, he points out that his studies suggest that

> The condition of entry (height of entry barrier) exercises an influence on profit rates which is distinguishable and separate from the influence of seller concentration. It is conceivable, of course, that high concentration and high entry barriers could be "intercorrelated" to such an extent that any industry that had one also had the other, so that we could only say that high concentration and difficult entry in combination were conducive to high profit rate. This, fortunately, is not the case, since among industries with "high" seller concentration (above 70 per cent control by 8 firms), we can identify industries protected by very different heights of entry barrier . . . The tentative indication is, therefore, that very high entry barriers provide an independent, contributing structural cause for monopolistic excess profits, and that the conjunction of high seller concentration and extreme entry barriers provides a less desirable structural situation than high concentration alone. Extremes both of seller concentration and of difficulty of entry may be tentatively viewed as at least quasi-independent characteristics of market structure which are conducive to unworkable performance in the matter of profits.[14]

Thus, following Bain, we will assume that seller concentration and barriers to entry are independent structural elements affecting seller average profitability. The question will be raised again in Chapter V, however, where the results of a multiplicative model will be offered for the reader's consideration.

Effects of Buyer Concentration

It was suggested above that the more effective is the coordination among sellers, the greater will be the average industry seller profitability. Several structural factors contribute to the effectiveness of seller coordination -- seller concentration, degree of product differentiation, cost conditions, etc.[15] Included also in this list should be the buying structure facing the industry.

Scherer points out that effective seller coordination

> is most likely when orders are small, frequent, and
> regular. It is least likely when requests for price
> quotations on large orders are received infrequently
> and at irregular intervals.
>   Any decision to undercut a price on which industry
> members have tacitly concurred requires a balancing of
> probably gains against costs. The gain from cutting
> turns on the increased probability of securing a prof-
> itable order. The cost follows from the increased
> probability of rival reactions driving down the level
> of future prices and hence reducing future profits.
> The gains from cutting are obviously greater when the
> order at stake is large relative to total sales than
> when it is small. Expected costs, on the other hand,
> probably rise less than proportionately with order
> size . . . Three or four departures in close succes-
> sion on $10,000 orders are more apt to trigger rival
> retaliation than undercutting the established price
> on a single, unusual million dollar order. Consequent-
> ly, the gains-cost balance will often be conducive to
> price cutting when a large order is at stake, while it
> will seldom be so for a small order, other things being
> equal.[16]

Stigler similarly suggests that "oligopolistic collusion will often

be effective against small buyers even when it is ineffective against

large buyers."[17]

Thus, a buyer, by appropriately spacing his orders, can sometimes

weaken a pricing agreement among sellers. But the buyer must be placing

orders that represent a significant fraction of the sellers' total sales

before he can have such an effect. The greater the fraction of sellers'

total sales controlled by one, or a few, buyers, the more power he (they)

can exert over the sellers. We can quantify this buyer power by formu-

lating a measure of buyer concentration, exactly analogous to the way we

quantify sellers' "monopoly power" (to set price and output) with an in-

dex of seller concentration. Thus, for a given level of seller concentration, the greater the buyer concentration, the less effective will be the sellers' efforts at coordinating their actions (i.e., seller collusion).

Increasing buyer concentration, however, not only leads to a weakening of seller collusive agreements, but also leads to an increasing possibility of "buyer collusion." Buyers would like to push for the lowest price a seller could offer -- i.e., the average cost, such that the seller reaped no economic profits -- but will settle for higher prices because of their uncertainty of the actions of other buyers. Suppose, for example, two buyers, A and B, both purchase from a given seller. If A is able to negotiate a price on his purchase sufficiently below the price paid by B, and the seller later experiences production problems resulting in delayed deliveries, A might fear that B will enjoy higher priorities and more favorable deliveries, since B's order is more profitable to the seller. Thus, A may be wary of trying to push the price too low. Furthermore, buyer overall costs increase as buyers themselves bid up the price they are willing to pay for their purchases. If buyers recognize their interdependence and coordinate in such a way as to refuse to pay prices above a given level, they can minimize their costs without fear of any one of them being disadvantaged with respect to the others.

Since the probability of successful coordination is related to the concentration of buyers in a manner exactly analogous to that of the probability of successful seller coordination being related to seller concentration, we see that seller and buyer concentration are both important elements of market structure, and the relationship between them has clear implications for seller conduct, and hence performance.

Bain identifies four types of markets with respect to the degree of buyer and seller concentration:

      1. fully atomistic markets
      2. ordinary oligopoly
      3. ordinary oligopsony
      4. bilateral oligopoly.

Of the latter he suggests that there will be

> express or tacit bargaining between buyer-seller pairs
> or between groups of buyers and sellers; and some gen-
> eral tendency for the power of large sellers and that
> of large buyers to offset each other so that price de-
> viates from the atomistic level less than it would
> with oligopoly alone or with oligopsony alone . . .
> <u>Comparative degrees of seller and buyer concentration</u>
> <u>should have some influence on the outcome.</u>[18]
>
>   (emphasis added)

He later points out that

> where it does occur, oligopsony has potential con-
> sequences more or less congruent with those of oli-
> gopoly . . . Express or tacit collusion among them
> (buyers) may grow up, and they may thus have a tend-
> ency to act jointly or collectively to exercise their
> monopsony (buyer's monopoly) power to depress buying
> prices and increase their own profit, generally at
> the expense of the sellers who supply them.[19]

Stigler[20] and Fellner[21] also explicitly comment on the power that
buyers can sometimes exert over sellers, while Scherer suggests that buyer
concentration in United States manufacturing is significant in only a few
special cases, and in general is not of sufficient magnitude to have any
appreciable effect.[22]

We can conclude, therefore, that at any given level of seller concentration, seller collusion will be less effective as the level of buyer
concentration increases, and that while we would expect seller profits to

increase with increasing seller concentration, all other things equal, we would expect them to _decrease_ with increasing buyer concentration.

Profits vs. Rate of Return

It will be necessary throughout this investigation to be explicit about the difference between rate of return and economic profits. Profit, P, will refer to the difference between the rate of return, R, and the cost of capital; i.e.,

$$R = P + \text{cost of capital},$$

where P is expressed as a ratio.

Since economic profits are zero for purely competitive industries in long run equilibrium, the competitive level of the rate of return would equal the cost of capital, and P can be interpreted as the "excess profit" reaped as a result of seller monopoly power.

The cost of capital is itself a constant plus an allowance for risk, under the assumption that it is appropriate for firms (and industries) to earn greater returns for undertaking ventures with outcomes that are less than certain. The greater the degree of uncertainty, the greater the risk, and therefore the greater should be the allowance and reward for undertaking that risk.[23] The constant, r, is referred to as the "risk-free" rate of return (the normal return for an investment whose outcome is certain), so that, therefore,

$$R = P + r + \text{risk}$$

The risk-free rate of return, r, can often be estimated from financial market information. But P is difficult to measure and is virtually never reported, and the risk premium, being a function of investors' perceptions, is an even more elusive variable to quantify. Therefore, most studies

evaluating the relationship between seller profitability and market struc-

ture are forced to utilize reported seller rate of return as a surrogate

for seller profitability. When this is the case, variations in P caused

by all elements of market structure, as well as all variations in the cost

of capital, must be controlled or accounted for.

Market Structure and Profitability

Nature of Previous Findings

The relationship between seller concentration and seller profitability

has been explored from many directions. Some authors have made the identi-

fication of this relationship the primary thrust of their efforts, while

others have included seller concentration as an exogeneous variable that

must be controlled in order to detect some other relationship that is the

main focus of their attention.[24] And the studies have varied in the level

of aggregation used, ranging from the firm level at the low end to the 2-

digit SIC level of aggregation at the high end. But if there is a funda-

mental association between seller concentration and seller profitability,

it has been an elusive one, for if the results of these studies are re-

markable for anything, it is for the non-uniformity of their conclusions.

With few exceptions, rate of return measures are used as surrogates

for profitability. Some authors have found little or no relationship be-

tween seller rate of return and seller concentration. Asch found that

seller concentration had little effect in explaining variations in seller

rate of return and concluded:

It appears that predictions of performance based solely on concentration may be improved substantially when other structural elements are introduced as explanatory variables. This may indicate that concentration is not a predominant structural determinant of certain performance patterns; or, more mundanely, that present measures of concentration (or definitions of industries) are deficient. Whatever the interpretation, it seems evident that there are serious limitations to the practice of using concentration as a proxy for industry structure or the "state of competition."[25]

Sato summarized his study by pointing out,

A similar comparison among a number of selected sectors of the economy seems to favor a hypothesis that the differential patterns of price-cost behavior are for the most part governed by differences in supply and demand conditions without making any reference to industrial concentration. A comparison of manufacturing firms making profits and losses points to limitations of demand as the most influential factor in determining differential price-cost relationships among them.[26]

Stigler[27] found a marginally significant relationship between seller concentration and rate of return, but when he adjusted his rate of return measure for excessive salary withdrawals by officers of smaller corporations, the relationship virtually disappeared.

Kilpatrick criticized Stigler's approach and made different adjustments for excessive officer salary withdrawals. He felt that the result of his study "strengthens the conclusion that greater concentration leads to higher profit rates."[28]

Several others have found statistically significant relationships between seller concentration and rate of return,[29] but not always at the same level of significance nor for the same time period. Levinson, for example, exploring the relationship annually over the time period 1947-1958, found correlation coefficients ranging from .07 to .76, with a median

value of .53.[30] Gambles, in a relatively thorough study, found similar
relationships over the time period 1947-1967, and showed that the annual
relationship was significantly related to general economic conditions (as
reflected in, for example, the unemployment rate).[31]

In addition to the differences in the statistical significance of
the relationship, the studies sometimes differ as to the nature of the
relationship found. Collins and Preston,[32] for example, found that their
profitability measure, P, was related to seller concentration, SC, and
other control variables, X_1, X_2, X_3, etc., by a non-linear relationship
of the form

$$P = fn(X_1, X_2, X_3, \text{ etc.}) - a(SC) + b(SC)^2$$

while two different studies by the Federal Trade Commission[33] found the
relationship to be

$$P = fn(X_1, X_2, X_3, \text{ etc.}) + a(SC) - b(SC)^2.$$

The partial derivatives with respect to seller concentration are different
in the two cases.

Bain,[34] Mann,[35] and Schwartzman[36] have detected a "threshhold" effect,
i.e., seller concentration is not an important factor in explaining variations in seller rate of return if it is very low, but there is a critical
point, near 50% (the exact point depends on the study and measure of concentration used), for which the effects of seller concentration become
much more pronounced.

Collins and Preston noticed the threshhold effect in one study, but
stated that "the apparent 'break' at the 50% concentration level vanished
if differences in capital intensity are taken into account."[37] In another

study they say, "We are therefore led to conclude that the association between concentration and price-cost margins revealed in this data may be described as continuous rather than discrete (dichotomous)."[38] In addition, Kamerschen,[39] in a study quite similar to Mann's, refuted not only the threshhold effect, but any relationship between seller concentration and rate of return.

Finally, some studies have found that the relationship between seller concentration and rate of return depends on the nature of the industries selected for study. Collins and Preston found a strong relationship (correlation = .51) between price-cost margins and seller concentration in consumers goods markets, but very little correlation in producers goods markets. They comment, "The difference in statistical results is striking in every case . . . Further, concentration is the only significant variable in the analysis of consumer goods industry data."[40] Sherman,[41] on the other hand, found significant relationships in both types of markets, and there was virtually no difference between the results for the two types.

Explanation of the Variation in Results

More important than the differences between studies, however, are the reasons for the differences between them. For if there truly is an association between seller concentration and seller profitability, the differences between the various (conflicting) studies can help illuminate that relationship.

The studies differ in several ways. First, they differ in the definitions of the variables used, particularly measures of profitability and concentration. Rate of return, usually used as a surrogate for profit-ability, often reflects net income, before or after taxes, as a per cent of net worth, sales, or assets, and is sometimes adjusted for capital structure, depreciation, and so on. It is typically based on Internal Revenue Service, Federal Trade Commission, or individual firm accounting data. In addition, Collins and Preston use a measure, "price-cost margin," derived from United States Census data.[42] Although it is not altogether clear what effects this variability might have, all the measures are so highly correlated that it is doubtful if any significant differences between studies can be attributed to differences in the definitions of profitability, particularly if industries are defined broadly, say at the 2-digit SIC level of aggregation. Sherman concludes:

> Empirically speaking, such high levels of aggregation are used here that it makes no significant difference in the conclusions whether the base is sales, equity, or total operating assets. Similarly, it makes no difference for the macroeconomic problem whether we define "profit" before or after tax, with or without interest, or with or without officer's compensation.[43]

Measures of concentration are less variable between studies; they have been defined as 4- or 8-firm concentration ratios based on value of shipments or assets. All except Gambles use the Census 4- or 8-firm ratios for 1954, '58, or '63, defined at the 4-digit SIC industry level, as a base, and formulate weighted average measures for higher levels of aggregation, weighting by value of shipments or assets. Gambles formulates a 4-firm asset concentration ratio using firm data combined with Internal Revenue Service industry aggregation data.[44] While some argue

that the measure of concentration used is quite important, and point out
the problems associated with relating Census concentration ratios, based
on Census defined industries, to rate of return figures based on Internal
Revenue Service or Federal Trade Commission industry definitions, most
authors suggest that reasonable measures of concentration are correlated
highly enough that the use of any one of them should be satisfactory.
Thus, it is likely that very little of the lack of uniformity of results
can be attributed to variations in the definitions of either the profit
measures or the concentration measures used.

A more important factor in explaining the non-uniformity of results
is the fact that the various studies apply to different time periods.
Gambles' study convincingly shows that the relationship between rate of
return and market structure is not a constant one through time. Using
his definition of seller concentration, he found simple correlation coefficients between seller concentration and rate of return ranging from
-.33 in 1947 to .64 in 1963.[45] Levinson,[46] too, found that the relationship varied through time. Consequently, those studies in which the profit
measure is an average over some period of time are likely (and do tend) to
exhibit higher correlations between profitability and concentration than
those that look at single, specific years; and two studies, using data
for different years, will not necessarily find comparable relationships.

While variability of the relationship through time can explain some
of the non-uniformity of results, it cannot explain all of it. Another
important factor is the level of industry aggregation chosen for the study.
As a general rule, studies at higher levels of aggregation, particularly
those in which industries are defined at the 2-digit, SIC level of aggre-

gation, have found more significant relationships than studies in which industries are defined more narrowly.[47] And with few exceptions, the studies in which industries are defined at the 4-digit level of aggregation have either failed to find a significant relationship at all between seller rate of return and seller concentration, or have found evidence of a non-linear relationship or a threshhold effect.

There are three possible explanations why higher levels of aggregation might lead to more significant results. First, in any study relating market structure to performance it is implicitly assumed that the industries used in the analysis are relatively homogeneous within the industries, and unrelated to other industries used in the study. This latter assumption is tantamount to assuming that the cross-elasticity of supply between any two industries is negligible, and therefore there is no potential competition between industries. But if the industries are defined too narrowly, there could quite possibly be some effects due to potential competition from producers in different, but technologically similar, product markets. Thus, a market would be more competitive than suggested by census concentration measures if firms in adjacent markets possess resource bases fluid enough to allow them to move into profitable opportunities, i.e., if there is a relatively elastic cross-elasticity of supply between two industries. Collins and Preston suggest

> One reason that concentration might be more closely
> associated with profitability between, rather than
> within, the principal sectors of an industry is that
> the competitive adjustments necessary to equalize in-
> terindustry profit rates are apt to be much easier
> within, rather than between the sectors. Thus, we
> might expect firms . . . to shift resources margin-
> ally from one textile industry to another, or from
> one machine industry to another, but much less
> readily from textiles to machinery.[48]

Aggregation to levels that include a large number of different, but technologically similar, industries, thus maximizing the technological differences between the industry observations used in the analysis, tends to
reduce the effects of potential competition. Thus, the effects of potential competition would become less important as we defined industries
more broadly (i.e., increased the level of aggregation), and therefore
higher levels of aggregation should lead to more sharply defined relationships between seller profitability and market structure.

The results of Collins and Preston support this conclusion. They
found significant correlations between seller price-cost margins and
seller concentration at the 2-digit level, but in only six of ten 4-digit
subgroupings. The six subgroupings in which significant relationships
were found were characterized by a relatively low degree of technological
similarity, so that potential competition between the narrowly defined
industries was minimal; in the remaining four subgroupings, the reverse
was true.

A second reason why higher levels of aggregation may lead to more
sharply defined relationships between seller concentration and seller
rate of return follows from a weakness in a fundamental assumption in the
regression model commonly used in these analyses. If we assume that seller
rate of return is related to seller concentration by the model

$$R = a + b(SC)$$

then we are implying that in purely competitive markets, _ceteris paribus_,
the reported (or measured) rate of return is equal to _a_ and in monopolistic markets the rate of return is equal to _a+b_ (if concentration is measured on a scale of 0.0 to 1.0). The coefficient of seller concentration,

b, then, is the amount of excess profit that would be available to a monopolist in an industry, and since all the observations in a regression model are assumed to be from the same (or identical) populations, it is implicitly assumed that this is the same for all industries used in the study. Therefore, the amount of excess profit available to a monopolist in any industry over the purely competitive level is assumed to be equal to b.

The assumption that all industries are characterized by the same purely competitive rate of return is not difficult to accept, for, abstracting from risk, growth, etc., the purely competitive rate of return in all industries is equal to the cost of capital, i.e., the risk-free rate of return. But to say that if all industries were monopolies they would all have identical excess profits equal to b is much more difficult to accept, for this places very severe restrictions on the relationship between the cost and demand curves in individual markets.

We cannot relax this assumption, for to do so would nullify the results of the regression analysis. For example, suppose industry A has a monopoly rate of return of a+b while industry B has a monopoly rate of return of a+2b. (Both have purely competitive rates of return equal to a.) Then a return of a+.5b is equivalent to a .5 level of concentration in industry A and a .25 level of concentration in industry B. Alternatively, a .7 level of concentration in each industry would lead to a rate of return of a+.7b in industry A and a+1.4 b in industry B.

Thus, in making the assumption that all industries have the same monopoly rate of return, a+b, we are "forcing" the model to operate around an average monopoly rate of return for all industries. At the very least this would lead to a higher percentage of unexplained variation in the regression model, reducing the significance of the coefficients and lowering the R^2, and at the worst the results of the analysis would be meaningless. But the effects of variations in available monopoly profits between industries would be maximum at the lowest levels of industry aggregation, where product markets are defined quite narrowly; and as we looked at higher and higher levels of aggregation (i.e., more broadly defined markets incorporating many specific product types), the variations would tend to average and cancel. Thus, the relationship between seller rate of return and seller concentration should become more sharply defined as we increase the level of aggregation.

Finally, if we wish to isolate the relationship between seller profitability (as opposed to rate of return) and seller concentration, the effects of other factors contributing to variations in both profitability and cost of capital (such as barriers to entry, product differentiation, business risk, etc.) must be controlled. The number of parameters chosen for control, the specific parameters chosen, and the surrogates used to measure them differ from study to study. To the extent that important parameters are excluded or improperly measured, the basic relationship looked for will be obscured. The effects of variations in important parameters will be most strongly felt across narrowly defined industry lines, but at more broadly defined industry levels, the effects of variations in these parameters will tend to balance out and cancel. Thus we would expect the relationship between seller profitability and seller concentration to be more visible at higher levels of aggregation if proper allowance is not made for other important determinants of the dependent variable used in the analysis.

This final point underscores the importance of controlling for the
other variables that may affect the relationship between seller rate of
return and seller concentration. The more important of these variables
would be the other elements of market structure affecting seller profitability, and those factors contributing to variations in cost of capital
between industries. Let us assume that the most important elements of
market structure are those first four identified by Caves (see above) and
add to those buyer concentration, thus:

1. (seller) concentration
2. product differentiation
3. barriers to the entry of new firms
4. growth rate of market demand
5. buyer concentration.

In addition, let the most important factor contributing to variations in
the cost of capital be differences in business risk between industries.
Thus, if we want to isolate the effects of seller concentration on seller
profitability, and utilize a regression model with seller rate of return
as the dependent variable, variations in seller rate of return caused by
the remaining five variables must be controlled. (See the mathematical
note, Appendix III.) Not one previous study has done this.

The most thorough study in this regard is Gambles'. His data generally suggests that when additional important elements of market structure
are included in a multiple regression analysis, the effects of seller concentration are isolated and determined more precisely.[49] But even Gambles'
data is weak in this regard since he has not controlled for variations in
all of the elements included above, and (as will be suggested below) we

might argue that the surrogate he uses for product differentiation is in-appropriate.

The one element of market structure that has been systematically ex-cluded from all studies is buyer concentration. If the number of buyers of a product are few, such that the purchases of each one represent a significant portion of the output for a seller, buyers can exact price concessions from sellers through threats of shifting patronage or through agreements among buyers not to pay more than some prearranged price. Thus, as buyer power increases, certeris paribus, we would expect seller prices, and hence seller profitability, to decrease. For example, if buyer power is measured by buyer concentration, then an industry char-acterized by a seller concentration of, say, 60% would reap higher prof-its if it sold to unconcentrated buyers than if it sold to markets char-acterized by high buyer concentration. Thus, seller profitability should be negatively correlated with buyer concentration.[50]

There have been few attempts at investigating the effects of buyer concentration on seller profitability, apparently for two reasons:[51]

> 1) a belief that it does not exist in sufficient magnitude to be important, and
>
> 2) it is quite difficult to assess buyer concen-tration quantitatively.

Nonetheless, at least two empirical results are consistent with the idea that buyer concentration may be more important than is generally realized. In one study, Stigler divided his observations into three rate of return groups (under 6%, 6-8%, and over 8%) and two groups characterized by "many buyers" and "few buyers." These latter designations generally corresponded to consumers goods and producers goods. Stigler noted that "no high rate of return industries dealt with few buyers."[52] Collins and Preston, in their study detecting a significant difference between seller profitability and seller concentration in producers and consumers goods markets, suggest, in part, that the "concentration-margin relationship is strongly affected by the balance of buyer-seller relationships across markets . . ."[53]

It is important to note that in consumers goods markets buyer concentration is held relatively constant by default, if we assume that in these markets buyers are atomistic and therefore buyer concentration is virtually zero. (This is an abstraction, since we are neglecting the effects that some large retailers, e.g., Sears, Roebuck, and so on, might have on manufacturers.) But in producers goods markets, buyer concentration is more variable, and if not controlled, the variations contributed by changing buyer concentration may obscure the significance of the relationship between seller profitability and seller concentration.[54]

We can conclude, therefore, with the observation that one of the fundamental factors contributing to the discrepancy of results in previous studies has been the lack of control for variations in important parameters that affect seller rate of return. If we relate seller profitability to only one or two market structure elements, we risk obscuring the very relationship we are searching for with uncontrolled variations in other important structural elements. In particular, a market element that has never been controlled is buyer concentration; and if buyer and seller concentration interact, as theory suggests they might, uncontrolled variations in buyer concentration could (and as we shall see in Chapter IV, do) have a very significant effect on the outcome of a regression analysis.

35

FOOTNOTES

1. Joe S. Bain, Barriers to New Competition, Their Character and Con-
    sequences in Manufacturing Industries (Harvard University Press,
    1956), p. 7.

2. Richard Caves, American Industry: Structure, Conduct, Performance,
    2nd Edition (Prentice Hall, Inc., 1967), p. 16. See also, F. M.
    Scherer, Industrial Market Structure and Economic Performance (Rand
    McNally, 1970), Chapters 3 and 4. Some authors argue that product
    differentiation is simply one of the barriers to entry. See, for
    example, Bain, op. cit., pp. 203-205.

3. See Joe S. Bain, Industrial Organization (John Wiley and Sons, Inc.,
    1959), pp. 29-30. See also Caves, op. cit., pp. 18-22; John C.
    Narver and Ronald Savitt, The Marketing Economy, An Analytical Ap-
    proach (Holt, Rinehart, and Winston, Inc., 1971), pp. 60-67; and
    Scherer, op. cit., pp. 186-192.

4. Bain, Barriers . . ., op. cit., p. 3.

5. Caves, op. cit., pp. 37, 38.

6. For examples of some of the theories that have been proposed see
    William J. Baumol, Business Behavior, Value and Growth (The Macmillan
    Co., 1959), esp. Chapter 3; or Donald Stevenson Watson, Price Theory
    and Its Uses (Houghton Mifflin Co., 1968), Chapter 20.

7. See below for a discussion of some of the more relevant studies that
    have been made.

8. See Caves, op. cit., pp. 18-21.

9. See virtually any book on price theory, or Scherer, op. cit., pp.
    145-152.

10. Bain, Industrial Organization, op. cit., pp. 276-281, and, more
    generally, Chapter 8. See also Almarin Phillips, "A Theory of In-
    terfirm Organization," Quarterly Journal of Economics, Vol. LXXIV,
    (November, 1960), pp. 602-613.

11. Bain, Industrial Organization, op. cit., footnote p. 273.

12. Ibid., footnote p. 279.

13. Ibid., p. 262.

14. Ibid., Chapter 9, quote on p. 415.

15. See Scherer, op. cit., Chapter 7.

16. *Ibid*., p. 206. See also George J. Stigler, <u>The Organization of Industry</u> (Irwin, 1968), Chapter 5, for a more extended discussion of the probability that a price cut will be detected and the net expected value to the price cutter of such an action.

17. Stigler, <u>op</u>. <u>cit</u>., p. 44.

18. Bain, <u>Industrial Organization</u>, <u>op</u>. <u>cit</u>., pp. 139-141. Scherer, <u>op</u>. <u>cit</u>., suggests six ways to classify markets, p. 242ff.

19. Bain, <u>op</u>. <u>cit</u>., pp. 150-155, quote on p. 150.

20. Stigler, <u>op</u>. <u>cit</u>., pp. 40-41.

21. William Fellner, <u>Competition Among the Few</u> (Alfred A. Knopf, Inc., 1949), pp. 17-28.

22. Scherer, <u>op</u>. <u>cit</u>., Chapter 9, especially pp. 240-241.

23. The idea that investors who accept greater risks are entitled to greater expected rewards is well developed in the field of Finance. See, for example, Wilbur G. Lewellen, <u>The Cost of Capital</u> (Wadsworth Publishing Co., Inc., 1969), pp. 11-18. There have been several empirical attempts at demonstrating the relationship between risk and return. See, for example, Gordon R. Conrad and Irving H. Plotkin, "Risk/Return: U.S. Industry Pattern," <u>Harvard Business Review</u>, Vol. 46, No. 2 (March/April, 1968), pp. 90-99 (appendix discussing their theoretical model in more detail is included with reprints ordered from the magazine); Paul H. Cootner and Daniel M. Holland, "Rate of Return and Business Risk," <u>Bell Journal of Economics and Management Science</u>, Vol. 1, No. 2 (Autumn, 1970), pp. 211-226; I. N. Fisher and G. R. Hall, "Risk and Corporate Rates of Return," <u>Quarterly Journal of Economics</u>, Vol. LXXXIII, No. 1 (February, 1969), pp. 79-92; and George J. Stigler, <u>Capital and Rates of Return in Manufacturing Industries</u>, a study by the National Bureau of Economic Research (#78), Princeton University Press, 1963.

24. For example, the main focus of the following studies is the identification of the relationship between market structural elements and seller profitability: Bain, <u>Barriers</u> . . ., <u>op</u>. <u>cit</u>.; Stigler, <u>Capital</u> . . ., <u>op</u>. <u>cit</u>.; Michael H. Mann, "Seller Concentration, Barriers to Entry, and Rates of Return in 30 Industries," <u>Review of Economics and Statistics</u>, Vol. XLVIII (August, 1966), pp. 296-307; and Norman R. Collins, Lee E. Preston, <u>Concentration and Price-Cost Margins in Manufacturing Industries</u>, (University of California Press, 1968), etc. On the other hand, the following studies incorporated market structural elements as control variables while studying other relationships that affect seller rate of return: David R. Kamerschen, "The Influence of Ownership and Control on Profit Rates," <u>American Economic Review</u>, Vol. LVIII, No. 3, Part 1 (June, 1968), pp. 432-447; Marshall Hall, and Leonard Weiss, "Firm Size and Profitability," <u>Review of Economics and Statistics</u>, Vol. XLIX (August, 1967), pp. 319-

331; and Matityaha Marcus, "Profitability and Size of Firm: Some Further Evidence," Review of Economics and Statistics, Vol. LI (February, 1969), pp. 104-107.

25. Peter Asch, "Industry Structure and Performance: Some Empirical Evidence," Review of Social Economy, Vol. XXV, No. 2 (September, 1967), pp. 167-182.

26. Kazuo Sato, "Price Cost Structure and Behavior of Profit Margins," Yale Economic Essays, Vol. 1, No. 2 (Fall, 1961), pp. 360-425.

27. Stigler, Capital. . ., op. cit.

28. Robert W. Kilpatric, "Stigler on the Relationship Between Industry Profit Rates and Market Concentration," Journal of Political Economy, Vol. 76, No. 3 (May-June, 1968), pp. 479-488.

29. See, for example, Leonard Weiss, "Average Concentration Ratios and Industrial Performance," Journal of Industrial Economics, Vol. XI, No. 3 (July, 1963), pp. 237-254; Victor R. Fuchs, "Integration, Concentration, and Profits in Manufacturing Industries," Quarterly Journal of Economics, Vol. LXXV, No. 2 (May, 1961), pp. 278-291; Harold M. Levinson, Postwar Movement of Prices and Wages in Manufacturing Industries, Study Paper No. 21, U.S. Congress, Joint Economic Committee, Washington, January, 1960; Howard J. Sherman, Profits in the United States (New York: Cornell University Press, 1968); Norman R. Collins and Lee E. Preston, Concentration and Price-Cost Margins in Manufacturing Industries (Berkeley and Los Angeles: University of California Press, 1968); Glenn C. Gambles, Structural Determinants of Profit Performance in U.S. Manufacturing, 1947-1967, unpublished Doctoral Dissertation, Department of Economics, University of Maryland, 1970.

30. Levinson, op. cit.

31. Gambles, op. cit., especially table, p. 87.

32. Norman R. Collins and Lee E. Preston, "Concentration and Price-Cost Margins in Food Manufacturing Industries," Journal of Industrial Economics, Vol. XIV (July, 1966).

33. Economic Report on the Influence of Market Structure on the Profit Performance of Food Manufacturing Companies, September 1969, Table 3-3, p. 25 and Table 3-4, p. 27; and The Structure of Food Manufacturing, Technical Study No. 8, National Committee on Food Marketing, June, 1966, Figure 13, p. 208. Both are Staff Reports of the Federal Trade Commission.

34. Joe S. Bain, "Relation of Profit Rate to Industry Concentration: American Manufacturing, 1933-1940," Quarterly Journal of Economics, Vol. LXV, No. 3 (August, 1951), pp. 293-324.

35. Mann, op. cit.

36. David Schwartzman, "The Effect of Monopoly on Price," The Journal of Political Economy, Vol. LXVII, No. 4 (August, 1959), pp. 352, 362.

37. Norman R. Collins and Lee E. Preston, "Price-Cost Margins and Industry Structure," Review of Economics and Statistics, Vol. LI (August, 1969), pp. 271-286.

38. Collins and Preston, "Concentration . . .," op. cit., pp. 105-106.

39. David R. Kamerschen, "The Determinants of Profit Rates in 'Oligopolistic Industries,'" Journal of Business, Vol. 42, No. 3 (July, 1969), pp. 293-301.

40. Collins, "Price-Cost . . .," op. cit., p. 278.

41. Sherman, op. cit.

42. See Collins and Preston, "Concentration . . .," op. cit., pp. 54-57 and Appendix A, Section 2, pp. 119-120.

43. Sherman, op. cit., p. 25.

44. Gambles, op. cit.

45. Ibid.

46. Levinson, op. cit.

47. For some examples, see Collins and Preston, "Concentration . . .," op. cit., Chapter 2, especially Table 11, pp. 46-47, and their discussion of the diversity of results between 2- and 4-digit levels of aggregation, pp. 109ff.

48. Ibid., p. 111. See also the notion of a "supply space" as it relates to interfirm competition developed in John C. Narver, "Supply Space and Horizontality in Firms and Mergers," Conglomerate Mergers and Acquisitions: Opinion and Analysis, St. John's Law Review, Vol. 44, Special Edition (Spring, 1970), pp. 316-340.

49. Gambles, op. cit. Compare the significance of the results for seller concentration between Tables IV-1, p. 68, and IV-3, pp. 89-90.

50. Powerful buyers sometimes use their strength to demand reciprocal purchase agreements rather than demanding lower prices. When this occurs, seller prices may not be depressed, but the prices paid for factors of production under such agreements may be inflated, so that the end result is the same. The theoretical link between buyer power and seller profits is not nearly so clear, however, when reciprocity occurs. See James M. Ferguson, "Tying Agreements and Reciprocity: An Economic Analysis," Law and Contemporary Problems, Vol. XXX (Summer, 1965).

51. See Scherer, _op. cit._, Chapter 9.

52. Stigler, _The Organization of Industry_, _op. cit._, p. 146.

53. Collins and Preston, "Price-Cost . . .," _op. cit._, p. 278.

54. It might also be argued that the relationship found in consumers goods markets is a spurious one, and that seller concentration in these markets is acting as a surrogate for product differentiation. While product differentiation is an important variable that should be included in any analysis of the effects of market structure, it is unlikely that its exclusion would lead to results such as found by Collins and Preston. That is, it is unlikely that a spurious correlation would lead to such extreme differences in the significance of the seller concentration term in the two types of markets.

CHAPTER III

THEORETICAL MODEL AND MEASUREMENT OF DATA

In this chapter we will formally develop the model to be used in the investigation of the effects of buyer concentration on seller profitability, and describe the methodology used for quantifying the variables in the analysis.

Buyer and Seller Concentration

For simplicity, assume at first that seller concentration and buyer concentration are the only factors that affect the average profitability and rate of return of a selling industry (thus we are assuming that the cost of capital is a constant for all industries). At low levels of seller concentration, seller coordination is quite difficult, and the probability of one seller violating an implicit (or explicit) pricing agreement is relatively great, so that we would therefore expect to see few pricing agreements between sellers. Industry price and output would be approximately that which would be expected under the conditions of pure competition, and economic profits, therefore, would be minimized. Small changes in seller concentration would not be expected to have much effect at low levels of seller concentration, so the partial derivative of seller profitability with respect to seller concentration, $\partial P/\partial SC$, would be low. But at higher levels of seller concentration, where seller coordination can be more effectively employed, and therefore prices, and profits, will be higher (according to the theory outlined in Chapter II), it is reasonable to expect that an increase in seller concentration would lead to an increase in profits that would be greater than if seller concentration were low.[1] Thus, $\partial P/\partial SC$ is a function of seller concentration, and for a given level of buyer concentration might have a relationship similar to that shown in Figure 3-1.

At any level of seller concentration, seller profitability will be higher if the industry faces a low concentration of buyers than if the concentration of buyers is high. Therefore, as buyer concentration increases, $\partial P/\partial SC$ will decrease at every point, and $\partial P/\partial SC$ is therefore a function of both seller and buyer concentration:

$$\partial P/\partial SC = f(SC,BC)$$

The relationship would be similar to that shown in Figure 3-2.

A change in the level of buyer concentration, however, has a much greater effect if seller concentration is high than if seller concentration is low, because at low levels of seller concentration, seller coordination is so difficult that there is no pricing agreement to be undercut, and, therefore, there are little or no economic profits being made. Thus, we would expect the effects of buyer concentration on seller profitability to be a function of the level of seller concentration, or $\partial P/\partial BC = g(SC)$. But, finally, as is the case with seller concentration above, if buyer concentration is dominated by seller concentration, or if buyer concentration is very low, so that no buyer represents a significant portion of the sales of any seller, a change in the level of buyer concentration is liable to have negligible effect on seller profitability. Therefore, the partial derivative of seller profitability with respect to buyer concentration is also a function of both buyer and seller concentration, similar to that shown in Figure 3-3, or

$$\partial P/\partial BC = g(SC,BC).$$

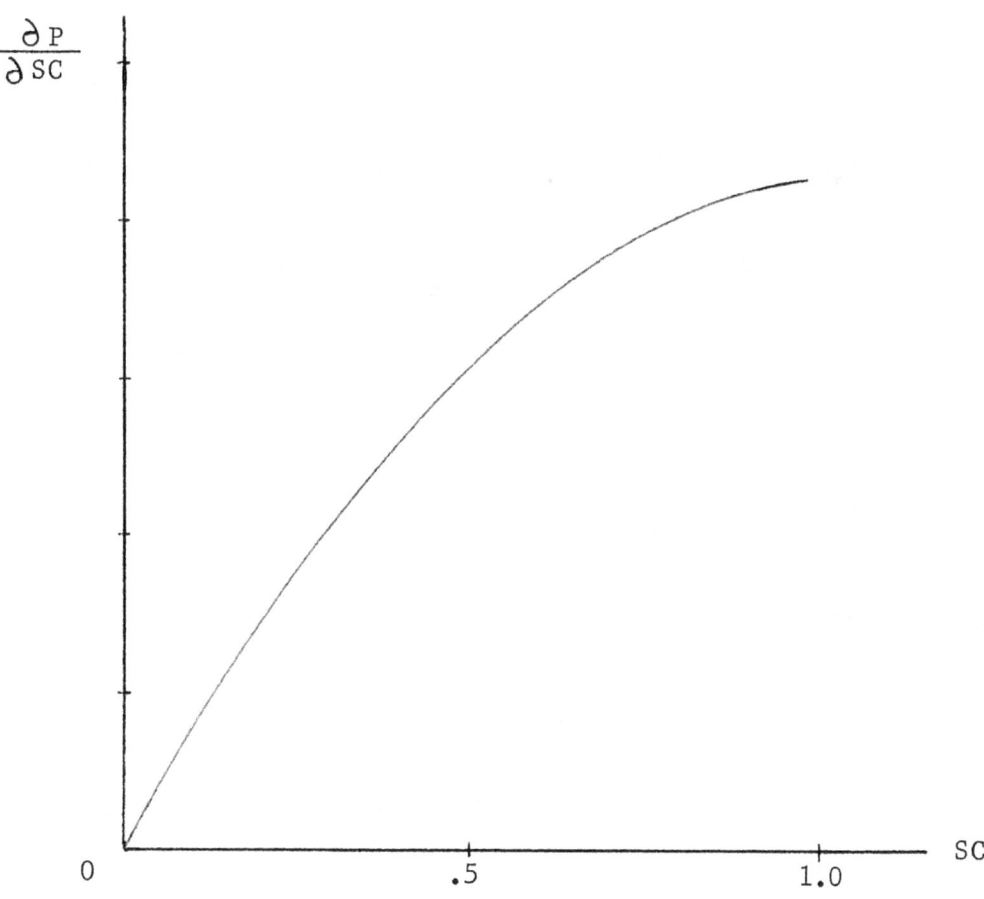

Figure 3-1

Relationship Between the Partial Derivative of Seller
Profitability With Respect to Seller Concentration
For Constant Buyer Concentration

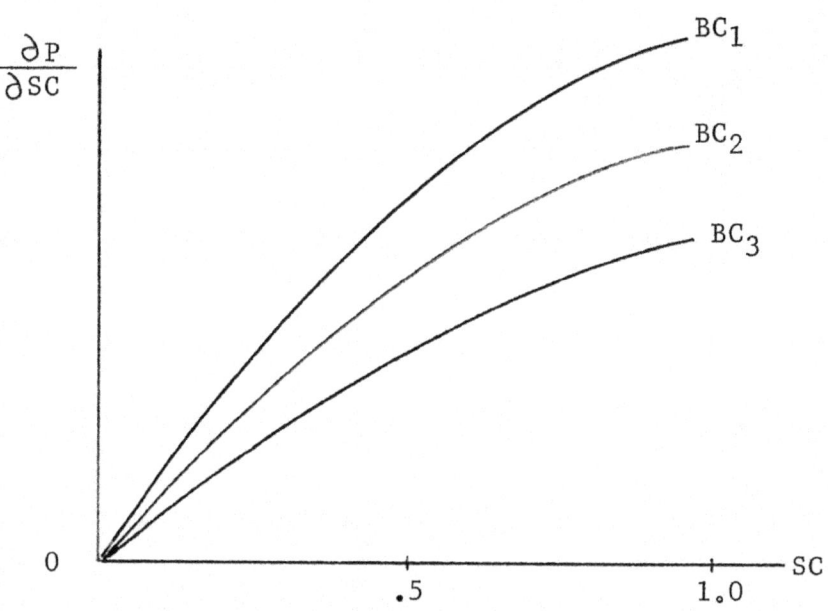

Figure 3-2

Relationship Between the Partial Derivative of Seller Profitability
With Respect to Seller Concentration as a Function of
Seller and Buyer Concentration
$BC_1 < BC_2 < BC_3$

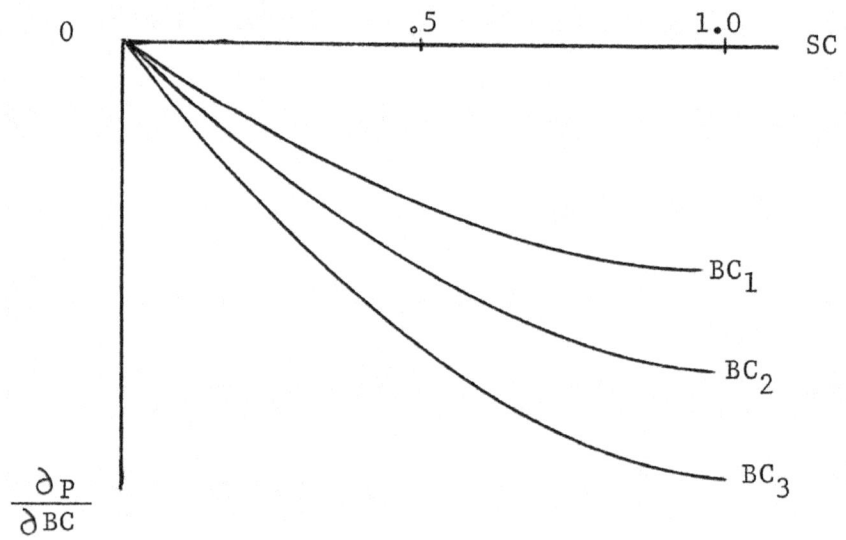

Figure 3-3

Relationship Between the Partial Derivative of Seller Profitability
With Respect to Buyer Concentration as a Function of
Seller and Buyer Concentration
$BC_1 < BC_2 < BC_3$

Thus, the relationship between seller profitability and buyer and seller concentration

$$P = F(SC,BC)$$

must be one such that[2]

$$\partial P/\partial SC = f(SC,BC) \qquad \text{(Figure 3-2)}$$

and

$$\partial P/\partial BC = g(SC,BC) \qquad \text{(Figure 3-3)}.$$

The function, F, meeting this requirement would be non-linear and quite difficult to use utilizing available statistical techniques. We can approximate F, however, with a linear model of the form

$$P = b(SC) + c(BC) + d(BC/SC)$$

where we would expect the sign of c, the coefficient of BC, to be negative. If we differentiate this function with respect to seller or buyer concentration, we get

$$\partial P/\partial SC = b - \frac{d}{SC}(BC/SC)$$

and

$$\partial P/\partial BC = c + \frac{d}{SC}$$

which are shown in Figure 3-4. This function is not identical to the desired one, particularly at the extremes of seller concentration, but it should be a reasonable approximation. In any event, it appears to be much better than the simple linear model that is commonly employed

$$P = b_1(SC) + c_1(BC)$$

(again we would expect c_1 to be negative) whose partial derivatives are

$$\partial P/\partial SC = b_1$$

46

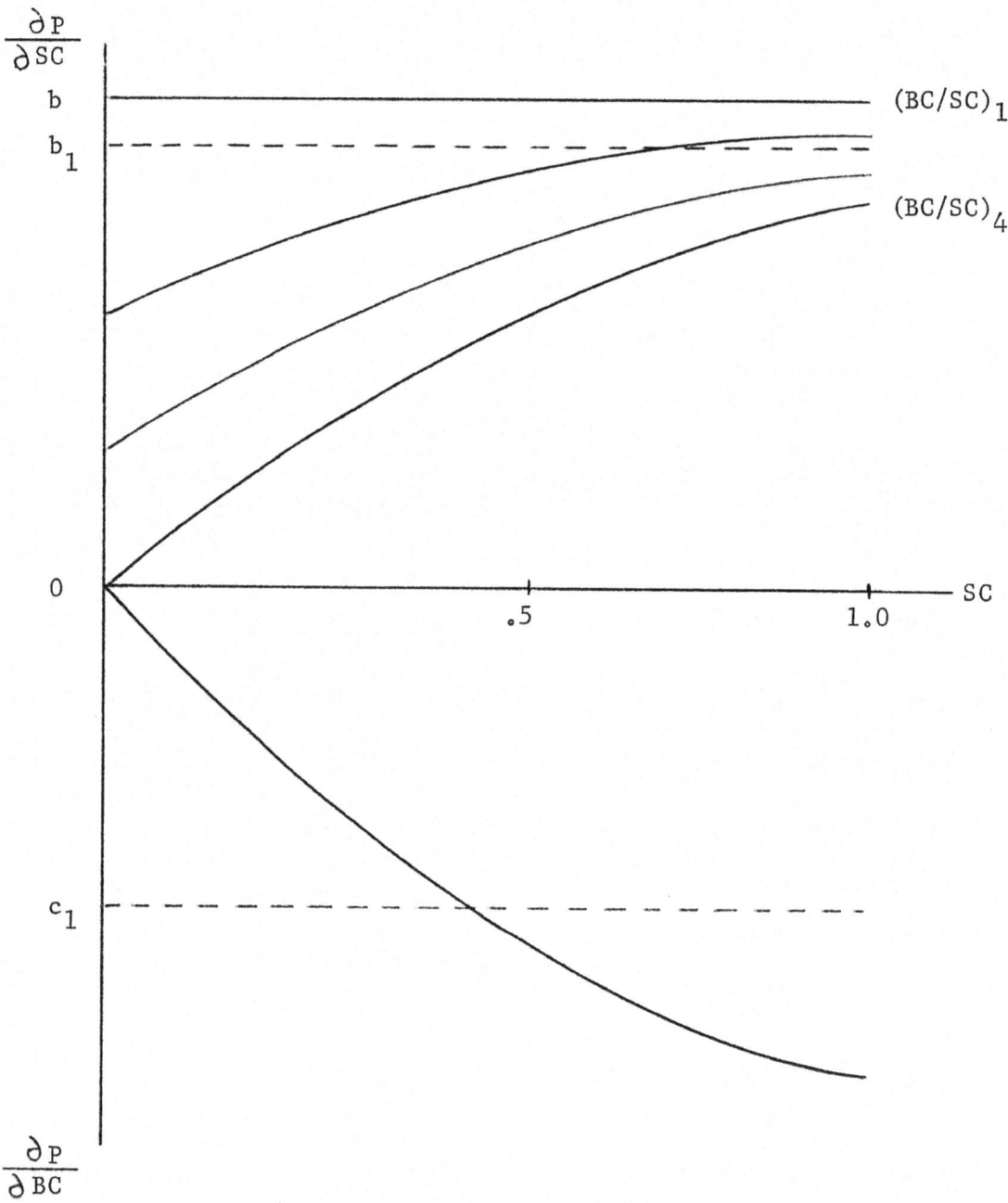

Figure 3-4

The Partial Derivatives of Seller Profitability With
Respect to Seller and Buyer Concentration For
the Model
$$P = a + b(SC) + c(BC) + d(BC/SC)$$
Where $(BC/SC)_1 < (BC/SC)_4$

and

$$\partial P/\partial BC = c_1$$

where b_1 and c_2 are constants and are shown as dotted lines in Figure 3-4.

We can now identify the specific hypotheses to be tested in this investigation. They are:

A   Industry average seller profitability increases with increasing seller concentration, and

B   Industry average seller profitability decreases with increasing buyer concentration.

And both of these effects are assumed to be greater at higher levels of buyer and seller concentration than at lower levels.

If we assume that the relationship between seller profitability and buyer and seller concentration is of the form

$$P = b(SC) + c(BC) + d(BC/SC)$$

the next job is to estimate the coefficients, b, c, and d. We cannot determine them exactly, but we can estimate them using a regression model of the form

$$R = a + b(SC) + c(BC) + d(BC/SC) + e$$

where R is the seller rate of return and e is an error term. (The cost of capital, we recall, is still assumed for now to be a constant for all industries.) Thus, we can take the average rate of return, seller concentration, and buyer concentration for several industries and estimate the coefficients using standard regression techniques. (We must not overlook the implications of such an approach, however, i.e., that industries in which, say, BC equals zero and SC equals 1.0 all earn the same level of profit -- see discussion of this point in Chapter II.)

In order to use this regression model, we must develop measures for the three variables, seller rate of return, seller concentration, and buyer concentration. A great many measures for average rate of return have been proposed as the most appropriate for this type of investigation -- measures of income before or after taxes, with or without interest, as a percentage of assets, sales, or equity, etc. -- and each has its critics. Some go so far as to say that since industry variations in any measure of profitability could represent short-run disequilibrium rather than differences in the "degree of monopoly" between industries, no measure is appropriate.[3] Sherman discusses the differences between the various measures of profitability but concludes that since all the usual measures are so highly correlated, it really makes little difference which is used, particularly at the higher levels of aggregation.[4] Nevertheless, Sherman suggests that the best measure for the purposes herein is net income before taxes plus interest as a percent of operating assets, and it is this measure that is used here. The data is for the year 1963, and is taken from the Internal Revenue Service's Statistics of Income.[5]

The industries used in this analysis are United States manufacturing industries defined at the 2-digit SIC level of aggregation. The theoretical reasons for believing that this is the most appropriate level for analysis were outlined in Chapter II and hinge on the fact that the effects of potential competition and variations in the dependent variable used in the analysis caused by exogeneous factors are easier to control at that level.

Four-firm concentration ratios, i.e., the percentage of the industry output accounted for by the largest four firms in the industry, are published by the United States Bureau of the Census[6] for 1963 for industries defined at the 4-digit level. A 2-digit seller concentration ratio is derived by formulating an average, weighted by value of shipments, of the 4-firm concentration ratios for the 4-digit industries making up the more broadly defined 2-digit industry.

The measure of buyer concentration facing the sellers in an industry is more complicated. First, it is necessary to assume that the buying concentration in an industry is the same as the selling concentration for that same industry. This is equivalent to assuming that the production functions of all the firms in an industry are identical, and, therefore, every firm buys factors of production in the same proportions as its share of the total output.

If a selling industry sells to several other industries, the average buyer concentration it faces is defined as the weighted average of the buying concentration of each of the buying industries, weighted by the value of shipments sold to each of those industries. For example, if industry A sells shipments valued at x_1 to industry B, x_2 to industry C, and x_3 to industry D, and these industries are characterized by seller -- and therefore buying -- concentrations of c_1, c_2, and c_3, respectively, the buyer concentration facing industry A would be

$$\frac{x_1 c_1 + x_2 c_2 + x_3 c_3}{x_1 + x_2 + x_3}$$

Thus, we must derive a matrix showing the distribution of output from each industry to each of the other industries, which is, in essence, an input-output table. The table in Appendix I, derived from the 1963 Input-Output tables for the United States economy,[7] shows the distribution of output

for the 2-digit industries used in the study. The total output (measured

by value of shipments) of each industry sold to each of the twenty 2-digit

industries is shown, along with (1) the total output sold to the twenty

2-digit industries, (2) the total interindustry transfers, (3) total

output to final demand, (4) miscellaneous output accounted for by ship-

ments to governments, net exports, and adjustments for capital formation

and changes to inventory valuations, and (5) total output of each indus-

try.[8] The diagonal entries in the left side of the table show intraindus-

try transfers -- i.e., the total value of shipments by firms in an indus-

try to other firms in the same industry. The figures in parentheses in

each of the right hand columns represent the fraction that that entry

represents of the total industry shipments, except that the subtotal of

shipments to 2-digit industries is shown as a fraction of total inter-

industry transfers.

The buyer concentration facing an industry can be calculated in four

different ways. First, we can ignore all the output except that to 2-

digit manufacturing industries, and formulate a weighted average based on

just these twenty entries. This would constitute a measure of buyer con-

centration for interindustry transfers. (And since this represents a

fraction of total interindustry transfers for manufacturing industries,

since transfers to other sectors of the economy are ignored, the figure

derived this way is an estimate for the buyer concentration for total in-

terindustry transfers.) But such a measure not only ignores other sectors

of the economy, it also ignores the output to final demand markets, which

is an important component of the output of most industries. Thus, if we

assume that final demand markets are atomistic, such that they are characterized by a buyer concentration of zero, we can derive a second weighted
average based on the shipments to each of the twenty 2-digit industries
plus those to final demand. This measure is more representative of the
total output of most industries.

A disquieting feature of most input-output tables, however, is that
the diagonal usually contains the largest entries, i.e., the largest single
purchaser of goods shipped from SIC 20 (Food Manufacturing) is SIC 20.
Our model relating seller profitability to seller and buyer concentration
is at a loss to predict what will happen when an industry sells to itself.
Thus, a third measure for buyer concentration could be derived by ignor-
ing the intraindustry shipments within the selling industry, and consid-
ering only the remaining nineteen 2-digit industries. Finally, the fourth
measure would consider not only the shipments to the remaining nineteen
2-digit industries, but also the shipments to final demand markets.

(For the purposes of this study, all distributions of output other
than those to the twenty manufacturing industries used in the study and
to final demand markets are ignored. Adjustments to the data could be
suggested for handling such things as shipments to other sectors of the
economy and to governments, etc., but it is assumed that since these
twenty interindustry shipments and shipments to final demand markets
represent nearly 70% of the total manufacturing output (see Appendix I),
they are the most significant factors in determining buyer concentration
in manufacturing industries, and the measures obtained are therefore
reasonable estimates for the true levels of buyer concentration in these
markets. Since these measures represent such a high percentage of total

manufacturing output, subsequent refinements to the data are quite unlikely to change significantly the fundamental _relationship_ between
seller rate of return on the one hand, and seller and buyer concentration on the other.)

Of the four measures suggested above, the fourth seems the most
plausible and is the one used here. Regressions are run with the others,
however, in order to confirm that the buyer concentration measure based
on the shipments to the other nineteen 2-digit industries plus shipments
to final demand markets is the appropriate measure.

Barriers to Entry

To this point, we have assumed that seller and buyer concentration
were the only determinants of rate of return within a given industry. But
there are other factors that can affect industry rate of return (see Chapter II), and if we wish to isolate the effects of seller and buyer concentration, we must control for these other factors.

One important factor affecting seller profitability is the height of
the barriers to entry into the industry. As Bain points out in his clas-
sic work on barriers to entry:

> Seller concentration alone does not appear to be an
> adequate criterion for the workability of competi-
> tion, since high seller concentration seems to be
> connected with significantly different sorts of per-
> formance depending on the height of the barriers to
> entry.[9]

Bain defines barriers to entry as

> The advantages of established sellers in an industry
> over potential entrant sellers, these advantages be-
> ing reflected in the extent to which established sell-
> ers can persistently raise their prices above a compe-
> titive level without attracting new firms to enter the
> industry.[10]

Bain identifies three types of barriers that may exist: (1) economies of large scale operation, placing smaller firms at a disadvantage; (2) absolute cost barriers arising out of captive sources of supplies or protected patent or license rights, foreclosing other firms entirely or allowing them in only at a higher operating cost than established firms; and (3) product differentiation barriers giving the established firms a favorable market advantage. But among these three, Bain suggests that, "the main culprit in establishing excessive or very high barriers to entry would appear to be product differentiation."[11] Caves similarly believes that product differentiation is the most important barrier to entry; he says "Contrary to what you might expect . . . product differentiation plays the leading role."[12] While other forms of entry barriers appear in a few specific industries, they appear to be the exception, not the rule. It will be necessary, therefore, to control for differences in product differentiation barriers to entry between industries.

A major source of product differentiation is advertising.[13] The Federal Trade Commission reports, "According to studies of the Cabinet Committee on Price Stability, product differentiation created and maintained by advertising is a major barrier to entry in consumer products."[14] They quote Turner:

> If heavy advertising expenditures thus serve to raise
> the barriers to entry, the adverse competitive conse-
> quences are important not only because new firms are

> kept out, but also because frequently it is the pros-
> pect of new entry which serves as a major competitive
> restraint upon the actions of existing firms . . .
> entry will be made more difficult as a result of the
> barriers created through extensive advertising.[15]

They conclude by pointing out that "the comparison of industry sales and expenditures for advertising provides a good measure of the extent to which product differentiation is a barrier to entry in consumer goods industries."[16]

Thus, we can use the ratio of advertising to sales as a surrogate for product differentiation, and both advertising expense and sales data are available from the Statistics of Income. But it would be incorrect to use simply the advertising to sales ratio so obtained. Clearly, product differentiation created by advertising is a more significant factor in consumer goods markets, where the perceptions of consumers are affected to a greater or lesser degree by advertising, than in producers goods markets, where product specifications, quality, and the personal contact between the buying agents and seller representatives are more important factors differentiating suppliers. But a simple ratio of total advertising expense to total sales implicitly assumes that (1) all sales take place in consumers goods markets, or (2) advertising has the same effect in producers and consumers goods markets.

Thus, we make the following assumption: the measure of barrier to entry we are most concerned with is product differentiation created through advertising in consumers goods markets, as measured by the advertising to sales ratio appropriate for that market. In order to determine this measure, we recognize that the measured advertising to sales ratio, A/S (where A is the total advertising expense and S is the total sales), is the weighted average of the advertising to sales ratios appropriate for consumers and producers goods markets, weighted by the value of shipments to each of these markets, i.e.,

$$A/S = \frac{(A/S)_c \ (S_f) + (A/S)_p \ (S_p)}{S_f + S_p}$$

where
A/S = the measured advertising to sales ratio
$(A/S)_c$ = the measure of advertising to sales in consumers goods markets, the measure we are interested in
$(A/S)_p$ = the measure of advertising to sales in producers goods markets
S_f = shipments to final demand markets
S_p = shipments to interindustry transfers.

Thus,

$$(A/S)_c = \frac{(A/S)(S_f + S_p) - (A/S)_p \ (S_p)}{S_f}$$

The measures for S_f and S_p come from Appendix I, and A/S from the Statistics of Income data. Thus, if we can determine $(A/S)_p$, we can solve for the desired measure of barriers to entry $(A/S)_c$. We do not know $(A/S)_p$ exactly, but we can approximate it if we make a second assumption that the advertising to sales ratio appropriate for producers goods markets $(A/S)_p$, is a constant for all industries. While this is not an easy assumption to accept, it is nonetheless clear that, in general, advertising induced product differentiation in producers goods markets is less variable and is of lesser significance than that in consumers goods markets.[17] Therefore, our assumption leads to an approximation, but a better approximation than if we simply use the measured A/S without adjustment.

We can obtain an estimate for $(A/S)_p$ by noting that industry SIC 33, Primary Metals, is unique in that it has no output to final demand. It also has the lowest measured advertising to sales ratio. Thus, if we take the measured A/S for SIC 33 as being equal to $(A/S)_p$ for all industries, we can then solve for the desired measure of advertising to sales, $(A/S)_c$, for each industry. It is this measure $(A/S)_c$, that is used for product differentiation in the model, but the more conventional measure, the measured A/S, is also substituted for purposes of comparison.

Growth of Market Demand

It is sometimes suggested that the reported rates of return are not valid indicators of the degree of monopoly since rates of return above the competitive level could occur in a purely competitive market in the short run under disequilibrium conditions.[18] In particular, in the face of growing demand, new entry may always lag demand, and rates of return may therefore maintain a level constantly above the purely competitive level. The excess profits being earned would continually attract new entry, but due to normal lags, or frictions, in adjustment, the demand could increase sufficiently during the period that the new entrants are establishing themselves that the previous level of rate of return (and therefore the previous level of profits) is maintained even after the new entry has taken place. Thus, even though the industry might be characterized as being purely competitive, economic profits could still be earned as a result of the frictional lags in new entry.[19] Since this effect could be different for different industries, an adjustment for market or industry growth should be made in our model.

The measure of growth of market demand used here is the percentage change in real output between 1960 and 1966 (a period that straddles 1963, the year chosen for investigation). Real output is the value of shipments deflated by the price index.

Risk

Excess profits are defined as the profits above the normal competitive level, or the difference between the rate of return and the cost of capital. But since the cost of capital is equal to a constant plus an adjustment for risk (see above, Chapter II, and especially footnote 23, Chapter II), a given rate of return is consistent with any number of combinations of excess profit and inherent business risk. In order to control for this effect, a variable reflecting the riskiness of industries must be included in the model.

Let the cost of capital equal r, the risk-free rate of return, plus a risk premium. The risk premium is a function of the degree of uncertainty of the industry's future performance, as perceived by investors; specifically, the more uncertain is the industry's expected performance, the higher is the risk premium. If the investors base their estimates of expected uncertainty on the past performance of the firm, then the variability of previous (historical) rates of return can be assumed to be an indicator of expected uncertainty and therefore of risk. We will use the standard deviation of rates of return through time as our measure of variability, and let that be our surrogate for risk.[20]

If industry returns tend to have a lower bound, i.e., in good years they may be quite large, but in lean years they never tend to fall below some nominal level (say 0%), then there could be a natural bias between the average rate of return and the standard deviation of the rates of return through time. To adjust for this, we could divide the standard diviation of yearly returns by the average return over the same period. As with the measure of industry growth, the time period used here is 1960-1966, and both the standard deviation of yearly returns and the standard deviation of yearly returns divided by the average return for the period 1960-1966 are used as alternative measures of industry business risk.

Industry Size

We have now introduced control variables for all the elements outlined in Chapter II (p. 31 above). One other parameter, industry size, is often controlled in studies relating market structure to seller profitability, with mixed results and with dubious theoretical justification.

First, at the firm level, Baumol[21] suggests that large firms should have greater profits than smaller ones since large firms have the same opportunities for investments as smaller ones plus better access to capital markets, and therefore a lower cost of capital. Monsen, et. al.,[22] however, suggest that owner controlled firms outperform management controlled firms, since the goals of owners tend to be that of profit maximization while the goals of managers may take other forms. Therefore, since the largest firms tend to management controlled, we might expect to find that the difference between large firms' profits and smaller firms' profits is smaller than Baumol suggests.

It is important to note that these two arguments not only argue for opposite effects, but also operate through different mechanisms. Baumol suggests that large size results in lower cost of capital, therefore enabling large firms to earn higher economic profits than their smaller rivals at the same overall rate of return. Thus, a control variable for firm size actually controls for variations in the cost of capital. Monsen, et. al., however, suggest that larger firms (on average) tend to be satisfied with lower profits, and therefore lower rates of return, than their rivals (at the same cost of capital).

If there are significant economies of large scale, we might expect larger firms to be more profitable than smaller ones. But both Bain[23] and Stigler[24] suggest that there are few really substantial economies of large scale in most industries,[25] and, therefore, we would expect to see no relationship at all between seller profitability and size of firm caused by scale economies.

Not surprisingly, empirical results are equally uninformative. Hall and Weiss[26] suggest that firm size and firm profitability are positively correlated, but results determined by the Federal Trade Commission[27] suggest that, at least in food manufacturing industries, size is unrelated to profitability. Both Collins and Preston[28] and Marcus[29] give evidence that the relationship between firm size and firm profitability depends on the industry being studied, and will be different for different industries.

The extension from firm size to industry size is even more tenuous. Even if we assume that all industries are made up of the same number of firms (which is obviously not true) and that therefore the larger firms would make up the larger industries, we still have no strong theoretical basis for suggesting that industry variations in rate of return should be related to variations in industry size.

Gambles' results concerning industry size are inconclusive. In his analysis using yearly regressions of industry average rate of return on market structure variables industry size was sometimes positively associated with rate of return, sometimes negatively associated with rate of return, and sometimes not significantly associated at all.[30]

We thus conclude that it would be prudent to control for variations in industry size, but we admittedly do so without good theoretical justification, and we are therefore unable to predict the nature of the results we will obtain. If we find that industry size is a significant variable in the relationship between seller rate of return and market structure, it will be left to the reader to develop his own answer as to why and through what mechanism the relationship occurs, or to decide if industry size is, in fact, acting as a surrogate for some other variable with which it is correlated.

Our measure of size will be, simply, total industry assets for 1963, as reported in the Statistics of Income. Some have argued that reported assets are an unreliable indicator of size because the same amount of capital equipment, for example, would appear differently on a balance sheet depending on the time period in which it was purchased, depreciation methods used, whether it was leased or purchased, etc. But we assume here that across an industry, particularly at the 2-digit level, these effects effectively cancel and total industry assets should be an appropriate measure for use.

Final Model

The model for investigation, then, is

$$R = P + \text{cost of capital}$$

$$= P + r + \text{risk premium}$$

$$= a + b(SC) + c(BC) + d(BC/SC) + eX_1 + fX_2 + gX_3 + hX_4$$

where

R = the industry average rate of return

P = industry average profitability

r = the risk-free rate of return in a purely competitive industry (equals the risk-free cost of capital)

SC = industry seller concentration

BC = the buyer concentration facing the sellers in the industry

X_1 = a measure of product differentiation, the advertising to sales ratio appropriate for consumers goods markets, $(A/S)_c$ above

X_2 = a measure of the rate of growth of demand, the percentage change in real output between 1960-1966

X_3 = a measure of business risk, either the standard deviation of yearly returns over the period 1960-1966, or that measure divided by the average return for that same period

X_4 = a measure of industry size, total industry assets.

It is assumed that variations in the cost of capital are independent of variations in SC and BC and that therefore SC and BC only affect industry average profitability. The remaining variables are included (1) to control for other factors that might affect industry average profitability, and (2) to control for variations in the cost of capital between industries.

FOOTNOTES

1. It could be argued that the partial derivative of seller profitability with respect to seller concentration might be a constant at all levels of seller concentration. The position is taken here, however, that a 10% change in seller concentration would have a greater effect at moderate levels of seller concentration, say from 60% to 70%, than at low levels of seller concentration, say from 0% to 10%. The partial derivative, therefore, would be generally increasing over the range from 0% to 100%. This is consistent, also, with the results obtained by those observing a nonlinear or threshhold effect in the relationship (see Chapter II, above).

2. The functional notation f(...) and g(...) is used purposely to avoid any suggestion that there may be a symmetrical relationship between the effects of buyer and seller concentration. There is no _a priori_ reason to expect that either element is more important than the other, nor that they have more or less equal effects on seller profitability. See Scherer's discussion of this point in Scherer, _op. cit._, Chapter 9, especially p. 246.

3. For example, see Yale Brozen, "Significance of Profit Data for Antitrust Policy," or Sam Peltzman, "Profit Data and Public Policy," both in J. Fred Weston and Sam Peltzman, _Public Policy Toward Mergers_ (California: Goodyear Publishing Co., 1969).

4. See Sherman quote, p. 25.

5. _Statistics of Income . . . 1963, Corporation Income Tax Returns_, United States Treasury Department, Internal Revenue Service.

6. _Concentration Ratios in Manufacturing Industries, 1963_, prepared by the Bureau of the Census for the Subcommittee on Antitrust and Monopoly of the Committee on the Judiciary, United States Senate, in two parts.

7. _Input-Output Structure of the U.S. Economy: 1963_, United States Department of Commerce, 1969, Volume 1 -- Transactions Data for Detailed Industries.

8. For a discussion of how the 1963 Input-Output tables were constructed, see "Input-Output Structure for 1963," _Survey of Current Business_, Vol. 49, No. 11 (November, 1969), pp. 16-47.

9. Bain, _Barriers_ . . ., _op. cit._, p. 204.

10. _Ibid._, p. 3.

11. _Ibid._, p. 204.

12. Caves, _op. cit._, p. 29.

13. Scherer has an excellent discussion of the relationship between advertising and barriers to entry, and of the effects of barriers to entry raised through advertising on firm profitability. In his discussion he summarizes the findings of several important studies in this area. See Scherer, op. cit., pp. 95-100, 230-233, 341-345.

14. Federal Trade Commission, Economic Report . . ., op. cit., p. 11.

15. Donald F. Turner, "Advertising and Competition," an address before the Briefing Conference on Federal Controls on Advertising and Promotion, sponsored by the Federal Bar Association, Washington, D.C., June 2, 1966, p. 203, quoted in Federal Trade Commission, Economic Report . . ., op. cit., pp. 11-12.

16. Ibid., p. 11. It would be reckless to suggest that advertising induced product differentiation is the only important barrier to the entry of new firms. Rather, it is suggested that advertising induced barriers are more important than the others on a cross-industry basis, especially at the higher levels of industry aggregation used in this investigation.

17. For example, Caves notes, "Most manufacturing industries which sell to producers (i.e., producers goods manufacturers) are free of differentiation." (Caves, op. cit., p. 22.) In addition, Scherer states that, "There are definite economies of large scale promotion for product differentiation, notably in the consumers goods industries." (Scherer, op. cit., p. 95.) See also, William S. Comanor and Thomas A. Wilson, "Advertising Market Structure and Performance," Review of Economics and Statistics, Vol. XLIX, No. 4 (November, 1967), pp. 423-440, and especially pp. 424-427. It is significant that most references to advertising induced product differentiation refer specifically to consumers goods markets.

18. See note 3, this chapter. See also Stigler, The Organization of Industry, op. cit., Chapter 13. Note that Stigler suggests that continuous disequilibrium is a random effect and, as such, it would not be expected to be correlated with any market structure variables.

19. J. B. Clark, The Distribution of Wealth (New York: Macmillan Co., 1928), p. 71

20. It should be noted that this measure is not without its critics. See discussions concerning appropriate surrogates for risk in Conrad, op. cit., Cootner, op. cit., Fisher, op. cit., and Stigler, Capital . . ., op. cit.

21. Baumol, op. cit., Chapter V.

22. R. Joseph Monsen, John S. Chiu, and David E. Cooley, "The Effect of Separation of Ownership and Control on the Performance of the Large Firm," Quarterly Journal of Economics, Vol. LXXXII, No. 3 (August, 1968), pp. 435-445.

23. Bain, _Barriers_ . . ., _op. cit._

24. George J. Stigler, "The Economies of Scale," _Journal of Law and Economics_, Vol. I (October, 1958), pp. 54-71.

25. See also Scherer, _op. cit._, pp. 90-93.

26. Hall and Weiss, _op. cit._

27. Federal Trade Commission, _Economic Report_ . . ., _op. cit._, pp. 25-26.

28. Collins and Preston, "Price-Cost Margins . . .," _op. cit._, p. 280.

29. Marcus, _op. cit._

30. Gambles, _op. cit._, especially pp. 89-90 (Table IV-3).

CHAPTER IV

EMPIRICAL RESULTS

Now that the model and the variables have been specified, we are ready to test our hypotheses that seller profitability is positively correlated with seller concentration and negatively correlated with buyer concentration. The results will be developed by starting with the simplest models commonly employed in other studies, and working toward the model outlined in Chapter III, showing, at each stage of the development, how the results are improved.

Consider, first, the simplest model commonly employed:

$$R = a + b(SC).$$

When we estimate the coefficients using regression techniques, we obtain (t-value in parentheses),

$$(1) \qquad R = 4.47 + .16(SC) \qquad\qquad R^2 = 56.7\%$$
$$(4.86)$$

The coefficient for seller concentration is highly significant, at better than the .0005 level of significance.

A better model, however, is one that controls for the effects of barriers to entry, i.e.,

$$R = a + b(SC) + c(barriers).$$

The usual measure for barriers to entry is the measured advertising to sales ratio, A/S (see Chapter III), and when that measure is used as a surrogate for barriers to entry, we obtain as estimates for the regression coefficients:

$$(2) \qquad R = 4.61 + .12(SC) + .78(A/S) \qquad\qquad R^2 = 64.0\%$$
$$(3.34) \qquad (1.86)$$

The addition of A/S increases the R^2 for the regression and it is, itself, a significant variable (at the .05 level), while seller concentration remains highly significant. On the surface the results appear to be quite satisfactory, but that conclusion is misleading. The <u>decrease</u> in the t-value for seller concentration (the level of significance has decreased from better than .0005 to .005) is evidence for the fact that A/S is an inappropriate measure for barriers to entry; for if it were truly "doing its job" in "explaining" the effects of barriers to entry on rate of return, then the seller concentration variable would explain the effects of seller concentration on rate of return more precisely than in equation (1), and its t-value should <u>increase</u>. The lack of precision of the A/S surrogate actually obscures the relationship between seller rate of return and seller concentration!

It was suggested above that a more appropriate measure for barriers to entry is the measured advertising to sales ratio adjusted for that fraction of sales taking place in consumers goods markets, i.e., the parameter X_1 in the model of Chapter III. Consider the three equations:

$$(3) \qquad R = 3.93 + \underset{(4.74)}{.15(SC)} \qquad + \underset{(1.71)}{.16(X_1)} \qquad R^2 = 63.1\%$$

$$(4) \qquad R = 5.23 + \underset{(4.82)}{.16(SC)} - \underset{(-1.09)}{.04\ (BC)} \qquad R^2 = 59.6\%$$

$$(5) \qquad R = 5.36 + \underset{(5.18)}{.14(SC)} - \underset{(-3.01)}{.10(BC)} + \underset{(3.38)}{.30(X_1)} \qquad R^2 = 76.5\%$$

Equation (5) shows that the effects of seller concentration on seller rate of return are "explained" more precisely -- as evidence by the increase in the t-value for the coefficient of SC -- when the appropriate measure for barriers to entry is included along with buyer concentration.[1]

68

The partial derivative of seller rate of return with respect to either SC or BC is a constant in equation (5). But it was suggested in Chapter III that the partial derivatives should be functions of the level of seller concentration, and it was proposed that an interaction term, BC/SC, be used to adjust for this nonlinearity. When this variable is added to the model we obtain:

$$(6) \quad R = 4.25 + .17(SC) - .17(BC) + 2.57(\tfrac{BC}{SC}) + .30(X_1) \qquad R^2 = 80.0\%$$
$$(5.43) \qquad (-3.12) \qquad (1.64) \qquad (3.48)$$

It is significant that all the t-values in equation (6) are higher than in equation (5), again demonstrating the improved precision obtained by the model suggested in Chapter III. The coefficient for the interaction term is only significant at the .10 level, the coefficients for BC and X_1 are significant at the .005 level, and seller concentration is significant at better than the .0005 level of significance. Equations (1) through (6) are summarized for convenience in Table 4-1.

The measure for buyer concentration used here is the fourth of the four alternatives suggested in Chapter III. It is appropriate to try the others in equation (6) in order to demonstrate that we have used the correct one. Table 4-2 compares regressions based on the alternative measures of buyer concentration. In that table, the following bases for buyer concentration apply:

B_1: based on interindustry shipments to 20 manufacturing industries;

B_2: based on interindustry shipments to 20 manufacturing industries plus shipments to final demand markets;

TABLE 4-1

REGRESSIONS OF SELLER RATE OF RETURN ON VARIOUS MARKET STRUCTURE VARIABLES (t-values in parentheses)

Equation #	Const	SC	A/S	X_1	BC	$\frac{BC}{SC}$	R^2
1	4.47	.16 (4.86)					56.7%
2	4.61	.12 (3.34)	.78 (1.86)				64.0
3	3.93	.15 (4.74)		.16 (1.71)			63.1
4	5.23	.16 (4.82)			-.04 (-1.09)		59.6
-	5.00	.13 (3.32)	.70 (1.53)		-.02 (-.57)		64.8
5	5.36	.14 (5.18)		.30 (3.38)	-.10 (-3.01)		76.5
6	4.25	.17 (5.43)		.30 (3.48)	-.17 (-3.12)	2.57 (1.64)	80.0

TABLE 4-2

EFFECTS OF ALTERNATIVE MEASURES OF BUYER CONCENTRATION

Const	SC	X_1	B_1	B_1/SC	B_2	B_2/SC	B_3	B_3/SC	B_4	B_4/SC	R^2
2.74	.08 (1.32)	.14 (1.57)	.10 (1.25)								66.6
-.54	.19 (5.07)	.15 (1.80)		2.68 (1.73)							69.1
4.55	.18 (5.54)	.26 (2.65)			-.09 (-2.01)						70.7
5.25	.14 (4.16)	.22 (2.17)				-1.80 (-1.25)					66.6
5.53	.14 (4.05)	.18 (1.86)					-.04 (-.79)				64.7
-2.02	.23 (4.07)	.15 (1.76)						2.50 (1.70)			68.9
5.35	.14 (5.22)	.30 (3.40)							-.10 (-3.01)		76.6
5.22	.13 (3.71)	.23 (2.25)								-1.50 (-1.40)	67.3
-5.93	.44 (1.87)	.19 (2.08)	-.26 (-1.09)	7.81 (1.58)							71.3
3.21	.22 (3.92)	.24 (2.47)			-.17 (-1.74)	2.50 (.89)					72.2
-1.18	.25 (4.61)	.19 (2.27)					-.09 (-1.85)	3.68 (2.44)			74.7
4.24	.17 (5.43)	.30 (3.48)							-.17 (-3.12)	2.59 (1.64)	80.0

B_3: based on interindustry shipments to 19 manufacturing industries, excluding intraindustry shipments;

B_4: based on B_3 plus shipments to final demand markets -- the measure considered most appropriate;

B_i/SC: interaction term to adjust for possible non-linearities in the relationships.

It is clear from Table 4-2 that B_4, the measure considered most appropriate in Chapter III, is superior to the others.

Finally, our complete model includes control variables for growth of demand, business risk, and industry size. These variables should be included in order to isolate more effectively the effects of seller and buyer concentration on seller profitability. Table 4-3 compares the regressions obtained when these additional variables are added, and the results indicate that growth and size are significant variables, but risk, defined either way, is not.

Equation (10), which incorporates our first surrogate for risk, the standard deviation of yearly returns, is interesting. Although the coefficient for risk is not statistically significant, it is of the correct sign and its inclusion in the model apparently improves the precision with which we can estimate the effects of variations in SC, BC, and product differentiation (X_1). It is not clear whether this result is a spurious statistical anomaly or whether there are, in fact, differences in risk between industries at the 2-digit level and the standard deviation of yearly returns is an imperfect surrogate for these differences. In any event, since our measures for risk are not statistically significant, we will accept equation (9) as the best fit of our model outlined in Chapter III.

TABLE 4-3

REGRESSIONS OF SELLER RATE OF RETURN ON ALTERNATIVE FORMULATIONS OF THE MODEL

#	Const	SC	BC	BC/SC	X_1	Size	Growth	Risk$_1$ (SD)	Risk$_2$ (SD/R)	R^2
6	4.25	.17 (5.43)	-.17 (-3.12)	2.57 (1.64)	.30 (3.48)					80.0
7	4.50	.17 (5.56)	-.16 (-2.80)	2.27 (1.43)	.29 (3.37)	-.03 (-1.03)				81.5
8	3.45	.16 (5.63)	-.19 (-3.74)	3.02 (2.12)	.29 (3.77)		.03 (2.13)			85.0
9	3.67	.16 (6.53)	-.17 (-3.73)	2.67 (2.18)	.27 (3.90)	-.05 (-2.12)	.04 (2.92)			88.8
10	2.99	.17 (6.73)	-.17 (-3.89)	2.58 (2.03)	.28 (4.07)	-.05 (-1.78)	.04 (2.31)	.51 (1.21)		90.0
11	3.29	.17 (6.17)	-.17 (-3.62)	2.55 (1.86)	.28 (3.65)	-.05 (-2.01)	.04 (2.73)		2.10 (.39)	89.0
12	3.67	.15 (5.03)			.14 (1.66)	-.08 (-2.07)	.04 (1.89)			73.7

Critical Values of t (one-tail test)

					Significance Level		
df	.05	.025	.01	.005	.001	.0005	
12	1.78	2.18	2.68	3.06	3.93	4.32	
13	1.77	2.16	2.65	3.01	3.85	4.22	
14	1.76	2.15	2.62	2.98	3.79	4.14	
15	1.75	2.13	2.60	2.95	3.73	4.07	

Source: William C. Guenther, Concepts of Statistical Inference, McGraw-Hill Book Co., 1965, p. 294.

The coefficient for the growth term is about as expected, but special note must be taken of the negative sign associated with the coefficient for size. We pointed out in Chapter III that we could not predict the nature of the results when we controlled for variations in industry size. It is interesting to note, however, that the argument proposed by Monsen, et. al., was the only one that would suggest a negative correlation between the rate of return and industry size.[2] The results might be interpreted, then, as indicating that the effect that Monsen, et. al., argue for actually dominates the other hypothesized effects of industry size on seller rate of return.

Equation (12) is included for comparison; it is the same relationship as equation (9) without provision for the effects of buyer concentration -- i.e., the more traditional test of this model -- and is considerably inferior to equation (9). We can thus conclude that:

1) buyer concentration is a more important element of market structure than had heretofore been recognized, and

2) the inclusion of a term controlling for variations in buyer concentration can considerably increase the precision of a regression estimate of the relationship between market structure, and in particular seller concentration, and seller rate of return.

One last consideration: following the results of those authors suggesting a non-linear relationship between market structure and seller rate of return (see Chapter II), we assumed such a relationship and incorporated an interaction term, BC/SC, to adjust for the effects of non-linearity. It is instructive to examine equation (9), the complete test of our model, from this standpoint to see if it is consistent with our

74

expectations.

The partial derivatives of seller rate of return with respect to seller and buyer concentration are, respectively,

$$\partial R/\partial SC = .16 - \frac{2.7}{BC}\left(\frac{BC}{SC}\right)$$

and

$$\partial R/\partial BC = -.17 + \frac{2.7}{SC}$$

These relationships are plotted in Figure 4-1 over the range of the independent variable SC and should be compared with the expected results (Figure 3-4). The dotted lines are the estimates of the partial derivatives from equation (5), which omitted the interaction term and assumed a linear relationship. As the ratio BC/SC exceeds 1.0, there are values of concentration for which $\partial R/\partial SC$ is negative, an unrealistic result. But it should be remembered that the model proposed in Chapter III was an _approximation_ for the hypothesized non-linear relationship, and as such it might be expected to exhibit weaknesses near the extremes of the data. Thus, while we cannot interpret the results too literally, it is clear that the assumed relationships are strongly implied and supported by the data.

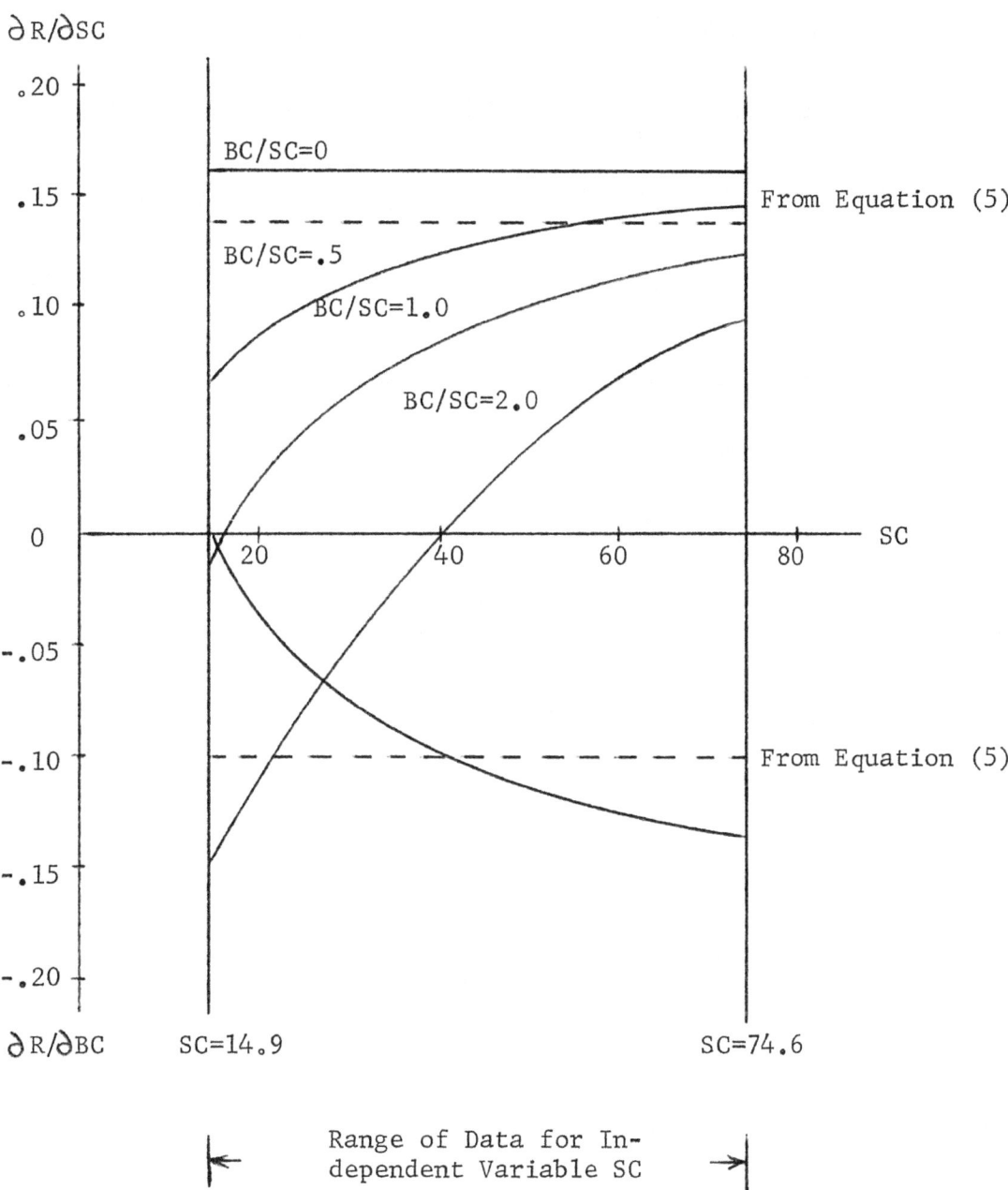

Figure 4-1

Partial Derivatives of Equation (9) With Respect to
Seller and Buyer Concentration Over the Range
of the Data For Seller Concentration

FOOTNOTES

1. If buyer concentration is added to equation (2), which incorporates the more conventional measure for barriers to entry, the results are much less satisfactory than those of equation (5):

$$R = 5.00 + .13(SC) - .02(BC) + .70(A/S)$$
$$(3.32) \quad (-.57) \quad (1.53) \qquad R^2 = 64.8\%$$

The lack of significance of the X_1 and BC terms in equations (4) and (5) is an accident of the data. Buyer concentration and X_1 are positively correlated, and since each has an opposite effect on seller rate of return, both must be included in the regression in order to separate their effects. See Appendix II for a table of 2-variable correlation coefficients and also the mathematical note in Appendix III.

2. See the discussion on the possible effects of variations in industry size on pages 58-60.

CHAPTER V

CONCLUSIONS AND DISCUSSION

Conclusions and Implications

The empirical test of our model strongly supports the hypotheses
formulated in Chapter III, i.e.,

> Industry average seller profitability increases with
> increasing seller concentration, and
>
> Industry average seller profitability decreases with
> increasing buyer concentration.

The implications of these results are substantial. First, and most important, buyer concentration is shown to be a highly significant element
of market structure, and has an effect on seller profitability equally
as strong as seller concentration if the relative magnitudes of the regression coefficients (in equation (9)) are any guide. Since the effects
of buyer concentration on seller profitability are directly opposite to
those of seller concentration, the exclusion of buyer concentration in
any study relating variations in market structure to variations in seller
profitability could obscure the real effects of variations in seller concentration. Comparison between equations (9) and (12) in Chapter IV shows
that in the model employed here the t-value associated with seller concentration increases by 30% when buyer concentration is included in the
regression. Thus, those studies referenced in Chapter II in which no,
or only marginally, significant relationships were found might well have
suffered from this exclusion.

Secondly, the results suggest that the relationship between market
structure and seller profitability is non-linear, and depends on the level
of seller concentration. The model developed in Chapter III is not suffi-

ciently sensitive to detect whether the non-linear relationship is smooth
and continuous, as suggested herein, or more abrupt, as suggested by the
concept of a "threshhold effect"; but we can safely reject (at the .025
level of significance, see Table 4-3, equation 9), the hypothesis that the
relationship is linear and does not depend at all on the level of seller
concentration.

Finally, barriers to entry, as measured by advertising intensity, is
shown also to have a significant effect on seller profitability. But advertising intensity should not be measured simply by the average advertising to sales ratio. Rather, an adjusted ratio should be formulated
which reflects the advertising intensity in consumers goods markets,
where advertising-induced barriers have a more significant effect. This
latter measure is shown to be more appropriate than simply the measured
advertising to sales ratio.

Review of Assumptions

It must be remembered, however, that the results are only as valid
as the assumptions on which they are based. We should discuss once again
the most important of these so that the results can be viewed in the
proper context.

Buyer concentration was defined as the percentage of the total output of an industry purchased by the largest four buyers. In Chapter III
it was assumed that buyers purchase in the same proportions as they pro-
duce, and therefore the buying concentration in an industry is the same
as the selling concentration for that same industry. Buying concentrations for 2-digit industries were derived from those for 4-digit industries

by a weighting process, and the buyer concentration facing a selling industry was derived by weighting the buying concentration of each of the purchasing industries by the value of the shipments to each of those industries. Shipments to final demand markets were assumed to be going to buyers characterized by zero buyer concentration, and the effects of shipments to governments, and to other sectors of the economy, were ignored. Clearly, then, the measure of buyer concentration is an approximation, and undoubtedly subject to some error. It must be left to the reader to decide if this measure for buyer concentration provides a realistic estimate of the effects that buyer concentration has on seller profitability; but it should be pointed out that if the reader believes that this measure is inappropriate and that there should be no relationship between this measure of buyer concentration and seller profitability, he should recognize that the results in Chapter IV have only one chance in approximately 1,000 of occurring by accident.

Secondly, in spite of Bain's assertion to the contrary (see Chapter II, p. 15), it might be argued that even a monopolist cannot earn economic profits in the long run if barriers to entry are zero. If entry is totally free, then any profits at all will attract new entrants. Consequently, an industry that has been highly concentrated for years, but one which has nevertheless been characterized by free entry, must have been earning, on average, only the opportunity cost of capital, but no economic profits that would attract new entry over these years. Therefore, it could be argued, the assumption that high levels of seller concentration lead to high levels of seller profitability presupposes some degree of barrier to entry. Yet our model (equation (9)) implies that the relationship between seller and buyer concentration affects seller profitability even if barriers to entry are zero.

We could postulate that a more appropriate model might be a multiplicative one of the form relating seller profitability to the product of seller concentration and barriers to entry, divided by buyer concentration, or

$$P \backsim \frac{(SC)^a (Barriers)^b}{(BC)^c}$$

This can be transformed to a model that is linear in form by taking the logarithms of both sides:

$$Ln(P) \backsim aLn(SC) + bLn(Barriers) - cLn(BC).$$

Regression techniques can be used to fit this model (substituting rate of return for profits and X_1 for barriers) yielding

$$Ln(R) = 1.17 + .31Ln(SC) + .11Ln(X_1) - .05Ln(BC)$$
$$(2.7) \qquad (2.6) \qquad (-2.0)$$

or

$$R = \frac{3.2(SC)^{.31}(X_1)^{.11}}{(BC)^{.05}}$$

with $R^2 = 60.0\%$. This result is not directly comparable to that of equation (6), however, since the dependent variable in the regression has changed (from R to Ln(R)), so all we can do is point out that this model is not free of problems either (suppose BC = 0), and leave the final decision up to the reader.

It could even be argued further that seller concentration and our measure for barriers to entry are really both imperfect substitutes for the true effects of barriers to entry -- that seller concentration, in

82

fact, has no effect on seller profitability, and that the variations in seller profitability are accounted for solely by variations in barriers to entry. There is, of course, no way to respond to this criticism except by reference to the assumptions, and our results and conclusions are only as good as those assumptions made in Chapter III.

Thirdly, we hypothesized that buyer and seller concentration affected seller _profitability_, but not _cost of capital_, and we were forced to use seller _rate of return_ as the dependent variable in the regressions. But suppose these two variables are not independent of the cost of capital. If seller concentration is positively associated with cost of capital, then our results overstate the effect that seller concentration has on seller profitability, since increasing seller concentration would lead to an increasing cost of capital and a decreasing economic profit for a given seller rate of return. But if increasing seller concentration leads to lower perceived risk, and hence a lower cost of capital, a more logical association, then our results _understate_ the strength of the relationship between seller concentration and seller profitability. Similar arguments hold for buyer concentration. Thus, if seller and buyer concentration are not independent of the cost of capital, and we then expect seller concentration to be negatively associated with, and buyer concentration to be positively associated with, perceived risk and, therefore, cost of capital, our results understate the true relationship between these market structure variables and seller profitability.

The two surrogates we used to control for variations in the cost of capital (the standard deviation of yearly returns and the standard deviation of yearly returns divided by the average return) both proved to have

82

Page 92

83

a statistically insignificant effect on seller rate of return. Therefore, we have implicitly assumed that the cost of capital for manufacturing industries is a constant at the 2-digit level of industrial aggregation. This might not be altogether unexpected, for if each 2-digit industry consists of a large number of product markets, and a larger number of firms, it is entirely possible that the effect of averaging at the 2-digit level is sufficient to cancel any differences in risk between industries. But it is also possible that significant differences in risk do exist between industries, and that neither of our two surrogates for risk are sufficiently sensitive to detect these differences. Thus, the positive relationship between seller concentration and seller profitability could be a spurious correlation actually reflecting the relationship between risk and rate of return. For this argument to hold, however, seller concentration and risk must be positively correlated -- an uncomfortable assumption. It would seem more reasonable to conclude, particularly in light of the strength of the statistical relationships obtained in Chapter IV, that seller concentration exerts an influence on seller rate of return that is independent of risk. Thus, if we have not controlled for the variations in risk between industries, our regression coefficients might reflect a slight bias; but it is not likely that the effects of uncontrolled variations in risk could result in a spurious relationship between other market structure variables and seller rate of return that appears as strong as that in equation (9) in Chapter IV.

If we interpret the results of equation (10) as indicating that our first measure for risk, the standard deviation of yearly returns, is in fact an imperfect measure of actual interindustry variations in risk, the

results of equation (10) also suggest that seller concentration exerts
an independent influence on seller rate of return. Under that interpretation, the equation shows that when the imperfect control for risk is
incorporated in the model, the effects of seller and buyer concentration
are isolated more precisely (although only slightly so) than in equation
(9), suggesting that a better surrogate for risk would have an even more
significant effect on the precision with which we can estimate the effects
of these variables.

Nevertheless, in accepting equation (9) as the best test of our
model, we have implicitly assumed that there are no differences in risk
between the industries used in this investigation. It is important to
differentiate between the conclusion that there are no _differences_ in risk
between industries, however, and that the industries are _risk-free_. For
example, if we determine the long run purely competitive rate of return
by extrapolating from equation (9), a dangerous practice since we are
then extrapolating beyond the range of the data (by substituting 0 for
all independent variables except BC/SC, which would equal 1.0) we find
that the purely competitive rate of return would equal 6.34%. From our
model in Chapter III we could then say that for the case of purely competitive industries in the long run

$$R = 6.34\% = P + r + \text{risk premium.}$$

Even if we assume a value for r, the risk-free rate of return, from financial market information, we still can say nothing about the relative
magnitude of P and the risk premium. All we can say is that since our
surrogates for risk were statistically insignificant, we have assumed P

and the risk premium to be constants for all industries.

Finally, we included a variable reflecting the growth of markets in order to control for the possibility that economic profits are possible in purely competitive industries in the face of significant growth of market demand (see Chapter III). Our growth variable is significant in equation (9), but the possibility still exists that it is an imperfect surrogate for market growth and that some of our relationships are in fact the result of spurious correlations with market growth.

In spite of these qualifications, however, the data speak quite strongly. In equation (9), the coefficient for seller concentration is highly significant, at much greater than the .0005 level of significance. The coefficient for buyer concentration is significant at better than the .005 level of significance. And the regression itself is significant at better than the .0005 level of significance (F=17.24). It is highly improbable that these results could have occurred by accident. Thus, while further studies may refine and qualify some of the assumptions made herein, it is unlikely that such refinements will alter the fundamental conclusions drawn regarding the relationship between buyer and seller concentration on the one hand, and seller profitability on the other.

Areas for Future Research

The analysis in the present study is at the 2-digit level of aggregation. It was pointed out in Chapter II that previous studies have generally found more significant results at this level than at the 3- or 4-digit levels, and some possible reasons for this effect were offered.

It is left to future research to determine if the inclusion of a control variable for variations in buyer concentration will improve the results obtained at lower levels of aggregation, or if the 2-digit level is, indeed, the appropriate level for analysis.

The relationship between market structure and seller profitability has been shown by Levinson[1] and Gambles[2] to be variable through time, and, in addition, Gambles has shown that such variation is related to general economic conditions. The development of the model in Chapter III would suggest that in periods of recession, when supply exceeds demand, seller coordination would be more vulnerable to buyer power, with higher probability of individual violations of seller agreements, than in periods of inflation. Thus, we might expect the coefficient of seller concentration to decrease in periods of recession and increase in periods of inflation. Similarly, buyer power would tend to be less effective in inflationary periods than in recessionary ones. Therefore, the coefficients for buyer and seller concentration might themselves be variables, each being a function of general economic conditions.

Yearly regressions should be run relating market structure to seller profitability, and the annual coefficients for buyer and seller concentration related to general economic indicators over the period examined. If such a relationship exists, its discovery would contribute enormously to our theoretical understanding of the dynamics of market structure, market conduct, and market performance.

FOOTNOTES

1. Levinson, _op. cit._

2. Gambles, _op. cit._ See also Chapter II.

SELECTED BIBLIOGRAPHY

BOOKS

Bain, Joe S. Barriers to New Competition, Their Character and Conse-
quences in Manufacturing Industries. Cambridge, Mass.: Harvard
University Press, 1956.

_____. Industrial Organization. New York: John Wiley & Sons, Inc.,
1959.

Baumol, William J. Business Behavior, Value, and Growth. New York: The
Macmillan Company, 1959.

Cassady, Ralph, Jr. Price Warfare in Business Competition: A Study of
Abnormal Competitive Behavior. Bureau of Business and Economic
Research, Graduate School of Business Administration, Michigan
State University, East Lansing, Michigan, 1963.

Caves, Richard. American Industry: Structure, Conduct, Performance.
Englewood Cliffs, New Jersey: Prentice-Hall, Inc., 1967.

Clark, John Bates. The Distribution of Wealth. New York: The Macmillan
Company, 1928.

Collins, Norman R. and Preston, Lee E. Concentration and Price-Cost
Mergers in Manufacturing Industries. Berkeley & Los Angeles:
University of California Press, 1968.

Fellner, William. Competition Among the Few. New York: Alfred A.
Knopf, Inc., 1949.

Ferguson, C. E. Microeconomic Theory. Homewood, Illinois: Richard D.
Irwin, Inc., 1969.

Levinson, Harold M. "Postwar Movement of Prices and Wages in Manufacturing Industries," Study Paper No. 21, U.S. Congress, Joint Economic
Committee, Washington (January, 1960).

Lewellen, Wilbur G. The Cost of Capital. Belmont, California: Wadsworth
Publishing Co., Inc., 1969.

McGuire, Joseph W. Theories of Business Behavior. Englewood Cliffs, New
Jersey: Prentice Hall, Inc., 1964.

Mueller, Willard F. A Primer on Monopoly & Competition. New York:
Random House, 1970.

National Industrial Conference Board. Concentration and Productivity. Studies in Business Economics, No. 103, 1969.

Scherer, F. M. Industrial Market Structure and Economic Performance. Chicago: Rand McNally, 1970.

Sherman, Howard J. Profits in the United States. New York: Cornell University Press, 1968.

Shubik, Martin. Strategy and Market Structure. New York: John Wiley & Sons, Inc., 1959.

Singer, Eugene M. Antitrust Economics: Selected Legal Cases and Economic Models. Englewood Cliffs, New Jersey: Prentice Hall, Inc., 1968.

Stekler, H. O. Profitability and Size of Firm. Berkeley: University of California Press, 1963.

Stigler, George J. Capital and Rates of Return in Manufacturing Industries. A study by the National Bureau of Economic Research. Princeton, New Jersey: Princeton University Press, 1963.

_____. The Organization of Industry. Homewood, Illinois: Richard D. Irwin, 1968.

_____. The Theory of Price. New York: The Macmillan Company, 1966.

Stigler, George J. and Kendahl, James K. The Behavior of Industrial Prices. National Bureau of Economic Research, General Series No. 9. New York: Columbia University Press, 1970.

Watson, Donald Stevenson. Price Theory and Its Uses. Boston, Mass.: Houghton Mifflin Company, 1968.

Weiss, Leonard W. Case Studies in American Industry. New York: John Wiley & Sons, Inc., 1967.

Weston, J. Fred, and Peltzman, Sam. Public Policy Toward Mergers. California: Goodyear Publishing Company, 1969.

ARTICLES

Asch, Peter. "Industry Structure and Performance: Some Empirical Evidence," Review of Social Economy, Vol. XXV, No. 2 (September 1967).

Bain, Joe S. "Relation of Profit Rate to Industry Concentration: American Manufacturing, 1933-40," Quarterly Journal of Economics, Vol. LXV, No. 3 (August 1957).

Bell, Frederick W. "The Effect of Monopoly Profits and Wages on Prices and Consumers' Surplus in U.S. Manufacturing," Western Economic Journal, Vol. VI, No. 3 (June 1968).

Bell, Frederick W., and Murphy, Neil B. "Impact of Market Structure on the Price of a Commercial Banking Service," Review of Economics and Statistics, Vol. LI (May 1969).

Collins, Norman R., and Preston, Lee E. "Concentration and Price-Cost Mergers in Food Manufacturing Industries," Journal of Industrial Economics, Vol. XIV (July 1966).

_____. "Price Cost Mergers and Industry Structure," Review of Economics and Statistics, Vol. LI (August 1969).

Comanor, William S., and Wilson, Thomas A. "Advertising and the Advantage of Size," American Economic Review, Vol. LIX, No. 2 (May 1969).

_____. "Advertising Market Structure and Performance," Review of Economics and Statistics, Vol. XLIX, No. 4 (November 1967).

Conrad, Gordon R., and Plotkin, Irving H. "Risk/Return: U.S. Industry Pattern," Harvard Business Review, Vol. 46, No. 2 (March/April 1968).

Cootner, Paul H., and Holland, David M. "Rate of Return and Business Risk," Bell Journal of Economics and Management Science, Vol. 1, No. 2 (Autumn 1970).

Ferguson, James M. "Tying Arrangements and Reciprocity: An Economic Analysis," Law and Contemporary Problems, Vol. XXX (Summer 1965).

Fisher, I. N., and Hall, G. R. "Risk & Corporate Rates of Return," Quarterly Journal of Economics, Vol. LXXXIII (February 1969).

Fuchs, Victor R. "Integration, Concentration, and Profits in Manufacturing Industries," Quarterly Journal of Economics, Vol. LXXV, No. 2 (May 1961).

Hall, Marshall, and Weiss, Leonard. "Firm Size and Profitability," Review of Economics and Statistics, Vol. XLIX (August 1967).

Kamerschen, David R. "The Determination of Profit Rates in 'Oligopolistic Industries'," Journal of Business, Vol. 42, No. 3 (July 1969).

_____. "The Influence of Ownership and Control on Profit Rates," _American Economic Review_, Vol. LVIII, No. 3, Part I (June 1968).

Kilpatric, Robert W. "Stigler on the Relationship Between Industry, Profit Rates and Market Concentration," _Journal of Political Economy_, Vol. 76, No. 3 (May/June 1968).

Lovell, Michael C. "Product Differentiation and Market Structure," _Western Economic Journal_, Vol. VIII, No. 2 (June 1970).

Machol, Robert E., and Lerner, Eugene M. "Risk, Ruin, and Investment Analysis," _Journal of Financial and Quantitative Analysis_, Vol. LI (December 1969).

Mann, H. Michael. "Seller Concentration, Barriers to Entry, and Rates of Return in 30 Industries," _Review of Economics and Statistics_, Vol. XLVIII (August 1966).

Mansfield, Edwin. "Entry, Gibrat's Law, Innovation, and the Growth of Firms," _American Economic Review_, Vol. LII, No. 5 (December 1962).

_____. "Size of Firm, Market Structure, and Innovation," _The Journal of Political Economy_, Vol. LXXI, No. 6 (December 1963).

Marcus, Matityaha. "Profitability and Size of Firm: Some Further Evidence," _Review of Economics and Statistics_, Vol. LI (February 1969).

Markham, Jesse W. "Market Structure, Business Conduct, and Innovation," _American Economic Review_, Vol. LV, No. 2 (May 1965).

Mason, Edward S. "The Current Status of the Monopoly Problem in the United States," _Harvard Business Review_, Vol. 62, No. 8 (June 1949).

Monsen, R. Joseph; Chiu, John S.; and Cooley, David E. "The Effect of Separation of Ownership and Control on the Performance of the Large Firm," _The Quarterly Journal of Economics_, Vol. LXXXII, No. 3 (August 1968).

Narver, John C. "Supply Space and Horizontality in Firms and Mergers," _Conglomerate Mergers and Acquisitions: Opinion and Analysis_, _St. John's Law Review_, Special Edition, Vol. 44 (Spring 1970).

Petermon, John L. "The Clorox Case and the Television Rate Structures," _Journal of Law and Economics_, Vol. XI (October 1968).

Phillips, Almarin. "A Theory of Interfirm Organization," Quarterly Journal of Economics, Vol. LXXIV (November 1960).

Sato, Kazuo. "Price Cost Structure and Behavior of Profit Margins," Yale Economic Essays, Vol. 1, No. 2 (Fall 1961).

Scherer, F. M. "Firm Size, Market Structure, Opportunity, and the Output of Patented Inventions," American Economic Review, Vol. LV, No. 5, Part I (December 1965).

Schwartzman, David. "The Effect of Monopoly on Price," The Journal of Political Economy, Vol. LXVII, No. 4 (August 1959).

Stigler, George J. "The Economics of Scale," The Journal of Law and Economics, Vol. 1 (October 1958).

Telser, Lester G. "Advertising and Competition," The Journal of Political Economy, Vol. LXXII, No. 6 (December 1964).

_____. "Cutthroat Competition and the Long Purse," Journal of Law and Economics, Vol. IX (October 1966).

Weiss, Leonard W. "Average Concentration Ratios and Industrial Performance," Journal of Industrial Economics, Vol. XI (July 1963).

UNITED STATES GOVERNMENT PUBLICATIONS

Federal Trade Commission. Economic Report on the Influence of Market Structure on the Profit Performance of Food Manufacturing Companies. September 1969.

_____. The Structure of Food Manufacturing. Technical Study #8, National Commission on Food Marketing. June 1966.

U.S. Bureau of the Census. Concentration Ratios in Manufacturing Industries, 1963. Prepared for the Subcommittee on Antitrust and Monopoly of the Committee on the Judiciary, United States Senate. Part I, 1966; Part II, 1967.

U.S. Department of Commerce. Input-Output Structure of the U.S. Economy: 1963. Washington, 1969 (3 volumes).

_____. "Input-Output Structure of the U.S. Economy: 1963," Survey of Current Business, Vol. 49, No. 11 (November 1969).

U.S. Treasury Department, Internal Revenue Service. Statistics of
    Income . . . 1963, Corporation Income Tax Returns. Washington,
    1968.

UNPUBLISHED MANUSCRIPTS

Gambles, Glenn C. Structural Determinants of Profit Performance in
    U.S. Manufacturing, 1947-1967. Unpublished Doctoral Dissertation,
    Department of Economics, University of Maryland, 1970.

APPENDICES

APPENDIX I

Distribution of Output for the Industries
Used in the Analysis

Table I-1 shows the value of shipments from each of the twenty 2-digit

manufacturing industries to each of those same industries plus, for each

industry,

1. the subtotal of value of shipments to manufac-
    turing industries

2. total value of shipments to all industries
    (total inter-industry transfers)

3. value of shipments to final demand markets

4. adjustments for

    (a) shipments to governments
    (b) capital formation
    (c) changes in inventory
    (d) net exports

5. the total value of shipments for each industry.

NOTES:

1. The supplying industries are read from the left column,
    and the distribution is read across the top of the table.

2. 0 means no shipments.

3. * means that there were shipments, but their value was
    too small to be of any significance.

4. Figures are in millions of dollars at producers' prices.

5. The figures in parentheses in each of the right-hand col-
    umns represent the fraction that that entry represents of
    the total industry shipments, except that the subtotal of
    shipments to 2-digit industries is shown as a fraction of
    total inter-industry transfers.

SOURCE:

Derived from Input-Output Structure of the U.S. Economy: 1963,
Vol. 1, U.S. Department of Commerce, 1969.

TABLE I—1

From: SIC	Industry	To: SIC 20	21	22	23	24	25	26	27	28	29	30
20	Food	12888	1	53	*	1	*	123	14	683	25	*
21	Tobacco	0	1764	0	0	0	0	*	0	0	*	0
22	Textile Mill	36	0	3686	9649	0	355	103	0	5	0	576
23	Apparel	127	0	2311	593	16	13	33	0	30	3	27
24	Lumber	97	6	0	8	3366	720	807	28	66	4	32
25	Furniture	*	0	3	2	21	177	*	18	*	0	3
26	Pulp & Paper	2040	126	242	145	46	90	4678	2721	852	163	214
27	Printing & Pub.	450	57	4	2	1	*	144	1808	35	1	2
28	Chemicals	562	86	2426	35	163	144	776	444	8359	667	2188
29	Petroleum	210	2	37	12	48	10	141	43	1333	1622	21
30	Rubber	254	*	106	126	14	343	196	72	431	2	445
31	Leather	3	*	2	60	3	6	2	*	5	2	18
32	Stone, Clay Glass	777	0	48	3	68	82	56	*	141	55	98
33	Primary Metals	3	0	*	6	87	325	33	8	472	51	74
34	Fab. Metals	2010	51	10	20	209	406	238	26	712	145	132
35	Non-Elect. Mach.	51	*	98	4	45	19	68	41	190	6	29
36	Elect. Machinery	8	*	0	3	3	22	3	2	34	*	26
37	Transportation Equipment	15	*	0	1	5	3	1	8	3	1	39
38	Instruments	9	1	13	15	4	21	20	140	66	2	17
39	Misc. Mfg.	8	*	61	352	18	13	6	30	39	3	65

TABLE I—1

31	32	33	34	35	36	37	38	39	Sub-Total	Total Inter-Indus.	Final De-mand	Adj.	Total Output
241	4	6	4	8	*	0	14	12	14077 (.66)	21306 (.29)	49921 (.67)	3036 (.04)	74263
0	0	0	0	0	0	0	0	*	1764 (.90)	1950 (.26)	4943 (.67)	532 (.07)	7425
227	31	24	47	15	23	146	61	153	15137 (.96)	15808 (.84)	2462 (.13)	579 (.04)	18847
42	34	28	27	32	32	450	8	22	3828 (.89)	4319 (.23)	14358 (.75)	479 (.02)	19155
43	100	62	133	73	45	192	8	160	5950 (.56)	10564 (.95)	230 (.02)	278 (.02)	11074
*	14	*	39	17	197	75	4	21	591 (.50)	1182 (.20)	3158 (.53)	1649 (.28)	5990
73	324	56	325	121	339	56	113	267	12991 (.82)	15798 (.88)	1315 (.07)	756 (.04)	17867
1	1	3	94	7	45	7	3	44	2709 (.22)	12285 (.75)	3160 (.19)	848 (.06)	16283
86	406	691	509	179	477	361	231	319	19109 (.77)	24782 (.71)	5827 (.17)	4109 (.12)	34749
6	120	239	80	126	109	130	12	23	4324 (.37)	11737 (.54)	8232 (.38)	1867 (.09)	21837
323	162	31	209	434	680	1052	148	308	5336 (.73)	7357 (.74)	1863 (.19)	753 (.06)	9891
888	3	7	11	21	3	2	8	48	1093 (.81)	1353 (.31)	3032 (.69)	9 (.00)	4394
2	1335	81	202	253	492	522	71	56	4342 (.37)	11581 (.93)	455 (.04)	744 (.04)	12480
7	157	10444	7463	4188	2665	5634	384	446	32447 (.86)	37600 (.97)	22 (.00)	1267 (.03)	38880
32	133	696	1522	1648	1500	3274	194	218	13176 (.58)	22645 (.89)	934 (.04)	1782 (.07)	25359
1	109	756	750	5951	1017	3207	130	28	12500 (.77)	16220 (.46)	659 (.02)	17965 (.51)	34944
*	39	301	296	1885	5900	1884	508	104	11018 (.70)	15802 (.47)	5870 (.18)	11755 (.35)	33457
*	8	147	352	741	428	15944	96	42	17834 (.82)	21849 (.37)	16410 (.28)	20982 (.36)	59241
23	6	31	118	175	352	525	447	14	1999 (.58)	3459 (.51)	1007 (.15)	2348 (.35)	6814
67	32	40	48	38	63	25	32	524	1464 (.49)	2983 (.42)	3327 (.47)	842 (.12)	7152

APPENDIX II

Two-Way Correlations Between the Variables Used in the Analysis

	R	SC	BC	BC/SC	A/S	X_1	Growth	$Risk_1$ (SD)	$Risk_2$ (SD/AR)	Size
R	1.000	.753	-.204	-.308	.636	.380	.410	.043	-.412	.024
SC		1.000	-.047	-.348	.543	.170	.301	-.149	-.475	.300
BC			1.000	.836	-.302	.522	.073	.256	.245	.088
BC/SC				1.000	-.377	.393	-.099	.274	.426	-.094
A/S					1.000	.463	-.106	-.272	-.509	-.150
X_1						1.000	.134	.073	-.198	.015
Growth							1.000	.248	-.057	.386
$Risk_1$ (SD)								1.000	.834	-.138
$Risk_2$ (SD/AR)									1.000	-.143
Size										1.000

APPENDIX III

Mathematical Note

Exclusion of Important Variables

When we say that we wish to isolate the effects of seller concentration on seller profitability, we mean that we would like to determine the partial derivative of seller profitability with respect to seller concentration -- the derivative of P with respect to SC, all other variables held constant. A simple regression analysis (simple correlation analysis) is the least meaningful approach in this regard, for if our model is

$$P = a + b(SC)$$

it is meaningless to talk about "all other variables held constant" when there are no other variables in the model.

As an illustration, let X_1 be the variable under study, and let us examine its effect on dependent variable Y. Thus we want to determine $\partial Y / \partial X_1$. Let variations in X_2, X_3, and X_4 also contribute to variations in Y, while all other variables, X_5 to X_k (where k is a large number), are relatively unimportant -- i.e., we can assume that $\partial Y / \partial X_i \approx 0$ for i = 5,6, . . ., k.

Now let Y be determined by the linear function

$$(1) \quad Y = \text{constant} + \frac{\partial Y}{\partial X_1} \cdot X_1 + \sum_{i=2}^{k} \frac{\partial Y}{\partial X_i} \cdot X_i$$

If we formulate a simple regression model,

$$(2) \quad Y = a + b(X_1)$$

then from (1)

$$\frac{dY}{dX_1} = \frac{\partial Y}{\partial X_1} + \sum_{i=2}^{k} \frac{\partial Y}{\partial X_i} \cdot \frac{dX_i}{dX_1}$$

and from (2)

$$\frac{dY}{dX_1} = b$$

Thus, the true partial derivative of Y with respect to X_1 (the quantity we wish to determine) is

$$\frac{\partial Y}{\partial X_1} = b - \sum_{i=2}^{k} \frac{\partial Y}{\partial X_i} \cdot \frac{dX_i}{dX_1}$$

We have assumed that X_2, X_3, and X_4 are also significant variables, and therefore $\partial Y / \partial X_2$, etc., are non-zero. Therefore, b could well be something different from the true partial derivative, except in the special cases where $\partial X_i / \partial X_1 = 0$ for i=2,3,4 (highly unlikely in any real world analysis), or where the terms in the summation happened to cancel, such that the value of the summation = 0.

Let us now define a different regression model,

$$(3) \quad Y = a + b(X_1) + c(X_2) + d(X_3)$$

(a and b are not the same as those in equation 2)

Then

$$\frac{dY}{dX_1} = b + c\frac{dX_2}{dX_1} + d\frac{dX_3}{dX_1}$$

If we make the simplifying assumptions (in general, not true) that $c = \partial Y / \partial X_2$ and $d = \partial Y / \partial X_3$, then it follows that

$$(4) \quad \frac{\partial Y}{\partial X_1} = b - \sum_{i=4}^{k} \frac{\partial Y}{\partial X_i} \cdot \frac{dX_i}{dX_1}$$

Thus, b in equation (3) still may not be the exact value we are trying to determine.

If we add X_4 to the regression model, making it

$$Y = a + bX_1 + cX_2 + dX_3 + eX_4$$

(a, b, etc. are again different here than in the previous equations)
the reader can verify that

$$\frac{\partial Y}{\partial X_1} = b - \sum_{i=5}^{k} \frac{\partial Y}{\partial X_i} \cdot \frac{dX_i}{dX_1}$$

and since it was assumed that $\partial Y / \partial X_i \approx 0$ for all i greater than 4,
this reduces to

$$\frac{\partial Y}{\partial X_1} = b$$

Thus, it is clear that the true effect of X_1 on Y, i.e., $\partial Y / \partial X_1$,
can only be determined if all variables having a significant effect on
Y are included in the regression. If we let Y stand for seller profitability, X_1 for seller concentration, and X_4 for buyer concentration,
the last example illustrates the fact that the coefficient in front of
X_1 may not be the true partial derivative of profitability with respect
to seller concentration unless buyer concentration is also included in
the model.

The exclusion of buyer concentration (or, indeed, the exclusion of
any important variable) can affect the results of a regression analysis
in two ways:

> (1) it can result in a reduced statistical significance
> for the coefficients included in the regression, if
> the value of the summation in equation (4) is approx-
> imately equal to zero, and, in addition

> (2) it can result in biased values for the coefficients
> if the value of the summation in equation (4) is
> something different from zero.

It is suggested in this dissertation that all previous studies have probably suffered from the former effect (and possibly from the latter), and that had all the important market structure variables been included in the previous analyses, the effects of seller concentration on seller profitability would have been demonstrated with much greater statistical significance.

Multicollinearity

The effects of multicollinearity among variables in a regression model can be explored using the above analysis. It is shown above (equation 4) that the regression coefficient, b, will be different from the true partial derivative if the value of the summation

$$\sum_{i=4}^{k} \frac{\partial Y}{\partial X_i} \cdot \frac{dX_i}{dX_1}$$

is different from zero. Now, multicollinearity means that two independent variables vary together, for example that dX_i/dX_1 has a finite value different from zero for some i. It is typically assumed that if the correlation between two independent variables is sufficiently high, then there can be problems with multicollinearity in a regression model. But from the above analysis it is clear that multicollinearity between, say, variables X_1 and X_4 may pose a problem only if

      (1) dX_4/dX_1 is not trivial

      (2) $\partial Y/\partial X_4$ is not trivial

and   (3) X_4 is not included in the regression model.

Under these three conditions, the term

$$\frac{\partial Y}{\partial X_4} \cdot \frac{dX_4}{dX_1}$$

in the summation can have a significant value, and will result in a significant error in the regression coefficient unless it is effectively cancelled by one or more other terms included in the summation.

(As a practical matter, multicollinearity has another effect. If two independent variables are highly correlated, the calculation matrix becomes singular and the determinant of that matrix approaches zero. Thus, rather substantial roundoff errors can result if intermediate calculations are not carried out to a sufficient number of places. Computer programs are particularly susceptible to this problem, especially when provisions for warning the user when such a condition exists are not built into the program. But this effect is purely one of mechanical technique, and would not be important if calculations were carried out with sufficient accuracy unless, of course, two independent variables were perfectly correlated so that the determinant of the calculation matrix was exactly zero.)

References:

Draper, N. R. and Smith, H. Applied Regression Analysis. John Wiley and Sons, Inc., 1966.

Rao, Potluri, and Miller, Roger L. Applied Econometrics. Wadsworth Publishing Company, 1971.

Snedecor, George W., and Cochran, William G. Statistical Methods. 6th Edition. Iowa State University Press, 1967, Chapter 13 and especially pp. 393-398.

APPENDIX IV

Basic Data Used in the Analysis

SIC	Industry	R (%)	SC (%)	BC (%)	BC/SC	A/S (%)	X_1 (%)	Growth (%)	Risk1 (SD)	Risk2 (SD/AR)	Size ($million)
20	Food	10.5	33.7	.9	.03	2.5	3.5	18.7	.90	.087	27.4
21	Tobacco	17.7	74.6	.0	.00	5.6	7.7	15.1	.57	.033	3.8
22	Textile Mill	7.9	32.7	16.6	.50	.6	1.9	16.2	1.66	.188	9.8
23	Apparel	7.8	16.5	6.8	.40	.9	1.0	55.3	1.35	.165	5.8
24	Lumber	7.4	14.9	27.8	1.86	.4	3.2	7.4	1.93	.282	6.1
25	Furniture	9.1	16.9	4.8	.28	1.1	1.3	32.0	2.58	.255	2.9
26	Pulp and Paper	8.8	30.7	26.7	.86	.8	6.2	34.1	.79	.080	11.7
27	Print. and Pub.	10.3	20.2	8.0	.40	1.1	4.0	43.7	1.58	.137	11.1
28	Chemicals	14.0	44.0	22.7	.52	4.1	19.8	54.7	.99	.069	29.1
29	Petroleum	5.7	33.8	10.1	.30	.5	.8	37.2	.69	.132	51.1
30	Rubber	9.3	34.9	28.7	.82	1.8	7.1	56.6	.78	.079	6.2
31	Leather	7.4	23.1	1.8	.08	1.2	1.5	11.9	1.47	.171	2.5
32	Stone, Clay, Glass	10.1	37.5	34.9	.92	.7	8.7	17.0	.51	.049	10.3
33	Primary Metals	6.9	47.7	39.3	.82	.4	.0	28.3	1.65	.208	30.1
34	Fab. Metals	9.2	24.4	40.9	1.70	.9	13.3	38.1	2.42	.236	14.1
35	Non-Elect. Mach.	11.1	35.0	45.6	1.30	1.0	14.6	49.3	2.94	.237	24.0
36	Elect. Machinery	9.5	45.0	21.4	.48	1.4	4.1	68.1	2.11	.195	18.8
37	Trans. Equipt.	17.6	62.4	3.8	.06	.5	.7	97.1	2.15	.142	33.9
38	Instruments	12.8	46.2	26.8	.58	2.3	9.0	47.1	3.15	.211	6.2
39	Misc. Mfg.	8.8	28.8	6.2	.22	2.0	3.5	5.6	1.90	.205	4.9

For definitions of variables, see Chapter 3.

Appendix V

Alternative Publications by the Author
How to Obtain Copies

Monograph: The San Diego State University Press published the dissertation as a monograph in 1973. This contained most of the same information contained in the dissertation, in a slightly more readable form. Its title was: "Market Structure and Seller Profitability, The Impact of Buyer Concentration." This publication has been out of print for a considerable time, although there are apparently a few libraries that still have copies available for loan.

Download a reprint from:
www.douglasbrooks.com/reprints/buyer1.pdf

Article: Finally, Brooks published an article in the "Industrial Organization Review," Vol. 1 No. 3, November 3, 1973, titled "Buyer Concentration: A Forgotten Element in Market Structure Models." This was an abridged copy of the same material from the dissertation. I have been unable to even locate copies of this journal, even in libraries, and to the best of my knowledge there are no sources for reprints of the article (except as noted below.)

The article has sometimes been mistakenly attributed to Douglas R. Brooks (instead of Douglas G. Brooks.)

Download a reprint from:
www.douglasbrooks.com/reprints/buyer2.pdf

VITA

Douglas Gordon Brooks, son of Ralph M. Brooks and Frances Green Huston, was born in Seattle, Washington, December 13, 1940. He received degrees of Bachelor of Science and Master of Science from Stanford University in 1963 and 1964, respectively. After employment as an electronics design engineer and as a technical marketing manager, he entered the doctoral program at the University of Washington in the fall of 1968.

www.ingramcontent.com/pod-product-compliance
Lightning Source LLC
Chambersburg PA
CBHW080704190526
45169CB00006B/2242